THOR RAMSEY

BROKE

I0164802

How Not To Give Up
When Climbing Out of Debt

Broke

ᴘ

How Not to Give Up When Climbing Out of Debt

Thor Ramsey

Pure Comedy Inc.
28900 Moonrise Way
Menifee, CA 92584

The names and other identifying characteristics
of some people in this book have been changed.

Pure Comedy edition published 2016 ISBN 978-0-9967-9640-8

First printing 2016

Printed in United States of America

Library of Congress Cataloging-in-Publication
Data Library of Congress Control Number: 2016930969
Pure Comedy Inc.

Ramsey, Thor
Broke: How Not To Give Up When Climbing Out of Debt
eBook ISBN 978-0-9967-9640-8
ISBN-13: 9780996796415
ISBN-10: 099679641X
1. Humor 2. Financial management 3. Debt
4. Christian living 5. Religion and culture
I. Title

Thank you for reading my book.

Go to www.thorramsey.com to sign-up for my blog and receive updates on special offers, new project news and exciting links to vacation get-aways and invites to my Tupperware parties.

Or, if you prefer, you can connect with me online:

Facebook - www.facebook.com/thor.ramsey
Twitter - @thorramsey

Pinterest (not really)

CONTENTS

To Marshall Allen, faithful friend and editor.
I hope this book finally pays for services rendered.

FREE INTRODUCTORY MATERIAL
(with Purchase of Book)

....

Right now I am not being paid. That's right. The initial advance for this book has been cashed, but I'm still writing to you, the reader, right now, free of charge. This material has been added to an already finished book. To what do you owe this good fortune? I simply want you to understand the point of this book.

If you're trying to climb out of debt or if you're thinking about starting that journey, then this book serves as the inspirational pick-me-up during the tough days, which after you count them, turns out to be all of them, give or take. So, what you won't find in this book are practical tips and proven strategies for surviving on graham crackers and Kool-Aid for thirty days. The point is, this isn't a self-help book. This is a help-me-God-because-I-can't-do-this book. Frankly, what you're going to need is encouragement, because climbing out of debt is a tough haul. These pages are here to provide you with the daily inspiration you need so you can follow the good advice of the financial gurus. After you read their books, this is the book to help you in your down times of trying to climb out of debt. It can be lonely and discouraging and you'll feel like quitting most days. So, hurry up and get started. That's what this book is for – those times when you feel like quitting. You know, like five-minutes ago. I'm right there with you in these pages. Think of this book as your own personal pick-me-up, the most encouraging book on being in debt ever.

Take comfort.

I've been there.

Still, I'm glad I'm not you.

1

HOW DID WE GET HERE?
(And Why Didn't My Wallet Come Along?)

♦♦♦♦♦♦♦♦♦♦♦♦♦♦

During the housing boom, my wife and I flipped four homes. We were debt free. We had money in the bank. We were ahead of the game. Then we renovated our kitchen.

Wow.

We have a nice kitchen.

No food.

But a great place to think about food.

We made some really, really, *really* bad decisions, which I discovered one day when I noticed we didn't have any money left. Our financial crisis was real. The economy took a nosedive (often referred to as a downturn, a less ominous word than nosedive) and work was less frequent than in boom time. I'm not so sure the job I have now is even considered work by many people. Most job conversations I have go like this:

"Whatta you do for a living?"

"I'm a standup comedian."

"Oh, that must be fun. How do you support your family?"

"How do I support my family? *I got 'em all britches!*"

The agency that booked my comedy shows imploded, owing me three months' worth of pay. We had no savings. We were in the hole with credit card debt. Our cash flow was kaput, which is a German word for "it's in the kitchen."

After deciding to take everything in-house instead of going with another agency, I started booking my own shows. Soon, I realized how my dependency was on the "agency" and not upon God.

Did I really believe that God was our provider? Two of the Ten Commandments reveal as much about God. The first commandment, which says, "Have no other gods before me," tells us that we have an all-sufficient God. Then, the eighth commandment says, "Do not steal," because God, being all-sufficient, is our provider. But what did my practice reveal about what I really believed about God?

I certainly believed the Lord sent us trouble when we needed it for the sake of our spiritual growth. The question I had now was, "Will he send a check?" One thing was certain: this financial struggle took the idea of praying for daily bread from belief to experience. The fear turned to, "What does daily bread mean to God?" You can get daily bread if you have a list of homeless shelters. My lack of trust made me think to myself, "Maybe we don't have a money problem. Maybe we have a trust problem."

As a married couple, we each played our part when it came to money. My wife handled the money and I ignored it. That's the nitty-gritty of going broke. I neglected to stay abreast of our financial situation, until there was a problem. I never even looked at our online account, because, quite simply, it was like homework. Then one day we looked at each other and asked, "How do we get out of this mess? If this keeps up, Capital One is going to keep us in for recess."

Naturally, in our search we turned to the experts. If you can find experts on TV, then, yes, we turned to the experts.

I bought lots of books by financial experts. I even read some of them. The ones who had TV shows. One of the books was by Suze Orman called, *The 9 Steps to Financial Freedom*. Her book was helpful.

Even though I never got past page 30, I did balance our checkbook. So, we're good for another three years.

Through the hand of Providence, I happened to have two complimentary copies of a famous financial guru's book. My wife and I decided to read them instead of fight.

It was a good decision.

But the hand of Providence? C'mon, Thor. Really?

Here's what happened (aside from minor embellishments):

Three years ago, comedian Taylor Mason and I toured 30 cities together. As we sat backstage during one of the shows, we were surrounded by hundreds of copies of this book on getting out of debt. They were piled everywhere. We couldn't sit down without sitting on a stack of books. Who says God isn't obvious? Planting an elbow on a pile of books, our conversation was filled with the things comedians discuss, like the tour, if it is worth continuing or not, some shows are well-attended, others not so much, etc. Money, debate, money, debate, future of tour, takes time to build an audience, etc. There we were, discussing money, sitting on a stack of books about financial planning. The pastor, a wiser man than either of us, gave us each a copy of the book.

It's like the old joke about a man who is stranded on an island and prays for God to rescue him. Then a ship comes along and offers to bring him aboard, but the man says, "No, thank you. I'm trusting that God will rescue me." Then a plane lands, one of those water-landing planes, and offers to give him a lift, but the man says, "No, thank you. I'm trusting that God will rescue me." Then a sub, really asking for directions, but offers him a ride anyway. Again, he declines by saying, "No, thank you. I'm trusting that God will rescue me." Finally, the man discovers a local tribe on the other side of the island, marries one of its inhabitants, a hot little number named Konocte, has ten kids, grows old and dies.

When he gets to heaven, the man asks God, "Why didn't you rescue me?" God says, "Are you kidding me? Do you really think that your bad decisions can hinder my will? Didn't you believe that all things work for the good to those who love me and are called according to my purpose? That whole shipwreck thing didn't catch me off guard. I know how thickheaded you are, that you'd reject every way off the island that came around. You became the butt of a good joke, thus fulfilling my purpose for you. Bad theology, but a good joke. The point is, sometimes my help is so obvious that you fail to see it. Yet, that doesn't prevent me from helping you. If the stupidity and sin of mankind could prevent me from doing anything I wouldn't be much of a God now would I? Besides, you wouldn't have met Konocte had you left the island. Wasn't she worth the price of living in a remote tropical paradise? Trust me, you wouldn't have been any happier back in Nebraska."

Or it goes something like that anyway.

So, I took the book home and never read it. I placed it on my bookshelf with every intent of forgetting about it.

About a year later I was at a conference where this financial guru gave a keynote speech and he gave the entire audience a copy of this same book. As it turns out, financial gurus tend to be extremely wealthy, probably because of that financial guru thing. Never one to turn down a free book, I took it home and placed it on my bookshelf next to the last free copy I'd received. If I can forget about it once, I'm sure I can forget about it twice.

Then it happened.

I was at my desk manning the phone, staring at things in my office while on hold when I noticed the two copies of this book. They were still sitting there on my bookshelf. I was reminded, "Hey, we're in a financial crisis. This seems like an ideal time to read them. One for my wife and one for me. Let's see who finishes it first. Winner take all.

Oh, that's right. We got no money."

Well, we read it anyway.

As we read it, we slowly faced the reality of our situation, the blood and guts of living from paycheck to paycheck with an irregular income, which makes things even more exciting. We began talking about money together, making financial decisions together, climbing out of debt together… but not without the help of God. "Thou shalt not murder" should always be highlighted in anyone's Bible during a financial crisis.

Or maybe that's just us.

My wife and I took inventory and discovered some of our financial fallacies, such as believing a budget means once we are out of money we can't buy anything else until we get some more money. That was our budget. Spend as much as you make.

Then there were the year-end tax receipts that revealed our spiritual attitudes. We didn't tithe ten percent. It was just above five percent. It felt like ten, but the receipts tell no lies. One statistic I heard said that the average American evangelical tithes about two percent to their local church. That says a lot about ushers. *Pass the plate, calculate, and if it's short pass it back. Do your job, guys!* It also says a lot about the heart of the American church. "Is it even mandatory to tithe ten percent? Aren't we under grace now?"

None of the financial gurus told us anything we didn't already know, which made us feel less dumb for losing all our money. We knew what to do. We just didn't do it. The gurus reminded us of that. *Then* we felt dumb for losing all our money.

Still, it must be asked, "If we knew what to do, then why didn't we do it?" That's the question that reveals the spiritual nature of money and that's the point of this book, to provide you the right inspiration so you can follow the advice of the gurus. After you read their books, this is the book to help you in your down times of trying to climb out of debt. It can be lonely and discouraging and you'll feel like quitting most of the time. That's what this book is for – those times when you feel like quitting. I'm right there with you in these pages. Think of this book as your own personal life coach that you can shut up at any time.

Maybe you're in the same situation we were.

It's time to take some drastic steps.

Here's the first step in my plan for recovery if you're broke: Buy another one of my books to give to a friend. I'm sure you know someone upside-down on their home loan. It's only half the country. This will be a great encouragement to them.

Good. Now that's out of the way, ask yourself this one simple question, "Do I know anybody *else* who might need a copy of this book? Anyone? Just one more person?"

Even though the light at the end of the tunnel was blocked by bills with bankruptcy peeking around the corner, we began this journey toward debt-free living (or at least getting out of debt for the time being). Many days we felt like giving up, but only if you count them all. We were doing it together, but we felt alone. That's when I decided to start writing about it. I wanted a detailed story of people like ourselves, a couple who follows a financial plan and makes hard decisions based on it, like skipping Starbucks once. *How did they find the courage to do it? What did they drink that day? Didn't they get a headache in the afternoon?*

I started keeping a journal of our progress and setbacks to feel less alone. Most people feel alone when they're climbing out of debt. To help people feel less alone, I decided to share the shame of our financial ruin with the world. My wife wasn't so crazy about the idea, but then I told her that a publisher will give us an advance for sharing our shame. And she still hated the idea.

Then I reminded her what the famous screenwriter and director Elia Kazan once said: "The writer, when he is an artist, is someone who admits what others don't dare reveal."

"Just don't let my mother see it," she said.

So, to amend Kazan: "The writer, when he is an artist, is someone who admits what others don't dare reveal – but not to his mother-in-law. No writer needs to be that stupid."

It's not an easy journey. It's not easy to maintain. I may have to read my own book again someday… next week… tomorrow.

There was no reason for us to be in this situation. Twice in the last five years we were completely debt free. We could be so far ahead. It's just beats you down when you think about it. So, you buy an issue *Guns & Ammo* and fantasize about owning a firearm on the day they come to evict you from your home and how that new couch you just charged will provide a nice barricade. Well, you go to the library anyway. Who has money for magazines these days?

Right now losing our home is only a distant fear in the back of my mind, which is probably why I sometimes wake-up at 5 a.m. and can't get back to sleep. I think that's what nightmares are – distant fears in the back of your mind. But if these distant fears aren't nightmares, then I don't know what to call them. Rational fears? That seems too... rational.

Sin?

Is anxiety sin?

From what I can tell "be anxious for nothing" is a command.

As we began our climb out of debt, I felt the tiniest bit of hope, a long hope delayed sometime in the future, but hope nonetheless. A hope without firearms involved. Because my wife and I read a book together, we were finally able to discuss money. We were on the same page.

Primarily because there was a page to be on.

We were reading a book.

I'm not sure what you call a book like this one where you learn from the tragedy of others. A comedy show? A "how not to" book? A Starbuck's Customer Manual? Maybe you've felt like the only other financial dupe on the planet. Take heart, you've found your leader. Few can top my idiocy. This is most definitely a "how not to" book, while at the same time being a "I walked that road too" book.

Broke chronicles our bad financial decisions and our climb out of the hole we dug. (By the way, you should only dig holes if you plan on filling them with treasure.) My editor asked me, "Are you sure you want to reveal all this?" But what ultimately is going to remain hidden? From a Christian standpoint, everything will one day come to light, even if you don't pay the electric bill. There's no use hiding if "everything is uncovered and laid bare before the eyes of Him to whom we must give account" – and this includes financial statements.

The truth is we all know better. If you want to get out of debt but feel hopeless and overwhelmed, that's where this book comes in. This book isn't about how to get out of debt. There are plenty of good financial gurus who have plans you can follow. This book is for the days you feel like quitting the guru's plan. This book shines some funny hope into your messy money life. You will read a chapter when you're feeling down and say to yourself, "If he can do it, surely I can do it." People want to know that other people are as dumb as they are – and, thankfully, I am. But it isn't just a problem of bad financial decisions. It is a spiritual issue, "for where your treasure is there your heart will also be,"[1] which I've found to be the key to all financial issues. Apparently, my heart was in overdraft. Whenever we talk about money, we're not really talking about money. It's really about your heart, about your spiritual state before the God of the universe.

I'm sure there's a spiritual reason to go to Starbucks daily.

I just haven't found it.

Yet.

This is messy and embarrassing stuff. It's not easy climbing out of debt, creating new money habits and turning your finances around. Our marriage suffered duress. Days and nights were filled with anxiety. Yet, in the midst of it all, I never gave up Starbucks. This alone showed my resolve to overcome the odds.

Don't you love happy endings?

---

1 Matthew 6:21

2

REAL ESTATE FUN PARK
(Featuring the Electric Loan Parade)

••••••••••••••

I like to do things around the house. It helps refocus my mind and it feels productive. This is something I do after I've just completed a creative project to reward my wife for her patience while I've been holed up somewhere writing (usually Starbucks) for weeks. It's also something I do when I'm depressed, which is when hammers are most useful. The point is, I restored much of our historic home myself, putting much of my own blood and sweat into it. Had I been better with a hammer, maybe there wouldn't be so much blood and sweat in our home.

I'm a do-it-yourselfer. I'm not really handy. I'm just cheap and determined. There's a store for cheap and determined people. It's called Home Depot. Maybe you've seen me at Home Depot. I'm the guy maneuvering a dust laden cart piled with tools and boards and placards of plywood and cement and tiles and peat moss... trying to go through the self-checkout lane. That irksome automated voice keeps telling me, "Please place the item back on the bin."

So, I scan it again.

"Please place the item back on the bin."

Scan.

"Please, place..."

"It's on the bin!" I yell at the machine.

Folks, if you can't check-it-out-yourself, you probably shouldn't do-it-yourself.

As you will see, both in home restoration and real estate wheeling and dealing, I am a do-it-yourselfer oblivious to the forces shaping me. Anyway, you should never wheel and deal in real estate, unless you're selling mobile homes.

When we bought our first home in 1998 the mortgage company required a 10 percent down payment, proof that we had $5,000 in savings and 7,000 box tops of our favorite cereal to make sure we were eating the most important meal of the day. Ten years later, buying our fourth home, the bank required a pen filled with ink, exactly no money down (and no less) and a "stated income."

If you aren't familiar with the ultra safeguarding system of the "stated income" that banks adopted during the housing boom, it went something like this:

"Do you ever get paid?"

"Yeah."

"Sign here."

That's all there was to it.

Thanks, Wall Street!

No one foresaw how this would soon entail a mass default of home loans. Well, a couple people foresaw, but no one on Wall Street listened to them.[2]

Wall Street is the center of American finance, the creamy filling of the United States economy. All those men and women shouting at each other in Oliver Stone films somehow affect whether you and I can buy homes. Is Wall Street alone to blame for all the front yards of foreclosed homes filled with overgrown plants? No, of course not. It's the gardener's fault. Other than weed killer, maybe the federal government played a small part.

But does the responsibility finally rest with the government?

---

2 You'll have to read Michael Lewis' book *The Big Short* to get the details.

Not in theory.

In theory, we are to blame because the government is "we the people." Thanks for the adjustable rate mortgage, Neighbor! Democracy is the theory anyway. Oligarchy seems more the reality sometimes. The rich get to make up the rules.

Our story illustrates what happened in America during the Almost Second Great Depression. During our bust, I started thinking about my part in this whole housing debacle, and that included my part as a Christian. I should have left well enough alone. The problem with introspection is that sometimes God lets you see your soul. Talk about *What Not to Wear*. I'll tell you what not to wear – your own righteousness, because you'll find out that it's filthy rags. And other spiritual lessons from reality TV.

The spiritual element to this whole housing mess is not pretty. It's spandex and a hot pink blouse. It's our financial soul. Okay, it's my financial soul. You'll have to search your own soul to find your own bad outfit analogy.

The year is 1998, right before bankers lost their minds, and our first home lists for $250,000. Just one-week after we sign the papers, the price for this same home in the same development soars by $25,000. One-week later and we wouldn't have been able to qualify for the home we just bought. That's like asking a girl out and a week later she becomes the homecoming queen. And you're not even part of the popular group.

Suddenly the most frightening experience of our lives turns into this exhilarating feeling that we made the right decision. We go from feeling uncertain about making the decision to buy a home to feeling like financial wizards who should be giving advice on a national radio show that televised. "Is the caller there?"

"Yes, Thor, should I borrow from my 401(k) or IRA to pay off debt?"

"The IRA? Aren't they are terrorist group?"

Okay, we just feel fortunate at first. The self-deception of feeling financially wise will come later when the bankers lose their minds, when the Deceitfulness of Riches calls out, "All-in."

Once you own a home, credit card companies, which you once saw as the enemy, seem loose and friendly. Every week we received some sort of incentive to charge something with convenience checks or a pre-approved credit card, an actual credit card just waiting to have some of that shine rubbed off.

All because we were now homeowners.

When we go to pick out cabinets and flooring for our first new home, people are lined-up outside the office of this housing development with lawn chairs and coolers, saving spots for some Disney-esque Electric Loan Parade, all waiting their turn to get in on the American Dream. We waltz past them all because we were here a week earlier, just ahead of the crowd, the wizards of cashola we begin to believe ourselves to be.

Four years later, that same home is worth $450,000. The housing boom makes us feel like the blessings will never cease. Real estate is a new ride at Disneyland. *You must be this rich to ride this ride.*

The problem with homeownership is that living in a home allows you more space to store the junk you buy. Don't get me wrong. Owning a home is a wonderful thing. Now I have a place to store my historic G.I. Joe collection.

The housing boom bamboozled banks, buyers and busters, the entire country blinded by the big sales event. And it all seemed quite legitimate because there were official papers and math involved. Once upon a time, you had to be rich to live in a half-million dollar home. Now, you just had to be dumb enough. (And I don't mean you in the sense of *you*, but in the sense of *me*.)

But do we stay in our first home for four years?

Oh, no.

We sell it after two years.

Why?

We can buy a bigger home, a nicer home with more rooms, higher end faucets and a third garage stall to house our cat's litter box, a dream come true for anyone with cats. Even cats get in on the American Dream during the housing boom.

When flipping homes became the fad (these days it's recommended that you flip coins) my wife and I flipped a home with another couple and came out just by skin of our chinny-chin-chin, not that my wife has a goatee, but just the same.

Our house flipping business all started with the home of an acquaintance who was in a must sell situation. I'll call him Bill (because he won't answer to that). His story is the same story as many during the housing boom in 2001. His mother-in-law cosigned his home loan. Did I mention he's divorced now? After Bill and his wife bought this home for $120,000 in 2001, they refinanced it twice to buy some necessity like stereo equipment for surround sound. So, their original $120,000 loan grew to around $200,000. That's what Abominable Credit Monsters do. They grow.

Bill's wife worked, but wasn't making enough to keep them out of the red so the bank gave them the option of losing their home or selling it. They decided to sell. And fast. Bill offered the home to my friend (who I'll call Mr. Chinny-Chin-Chin) and he declined because he didn't know anything about flipping homes. But after Mr. Chinny-Chin-Chin shares this with me, I can't stop talking about it. "It's real estate! Why let not knowing anything stop us? That's never stopped me from any do-it-yourself project. We could flip that house together and make a killing."

"I don't think we need to kill Bill to flip the home."

"No. Make a killing financially."

"How do you kill money?"

We *really* didn't know anything.

The thing that is most troubling in hindsight is that I didn't have an amazing grace attitude toward the misfortunes of Bill. I blamed his situation on him completely, not out loud during conversation or anything, but internally. Who can hear what anyone is saying with that surround sound he has? Later, Mr. Chinny-Chin-Chin and I decided to reconsider Bill's offer when we learned that another acquaintance of ours had stepped in and taken him up on it. I'll call him Punch, because that's what he beat us to. The home was no longer available for us to flip.

Punch was in real estate, so Bill trusted him. What Punch didn't tell Bill is that his home was worth a lot more than what Punch bought it for which is why Punch made $80,000 after flipping it. That's one side of it. The other side of it is that Bill was in a bad situation and needed to sell right away, a situation I have a lot more sympathy for now that I've gone broke myself. All I can say is, "That surround sound is amazing!" Even in a cardboard home.

But at the time, we kicked ourselves. Right in the Chinny-Chin-Chin. Since Mr. Chinny-Chin-Chin and his wife were renting a home when the market was still booming, I suggested we flip their home since their landlord wanted to sell it. Our credit was stellar, so my wife and I became the primary owners of Mr. Chinny-Chin-Chin's home and we went to work with fresh paint, new wood floors, sod in the backyard and flowers in the front. After paying our day laborers with a Kennedy Silver Dollar that they could split amongst themselves and whacking a "for sale" sign in the ground we were in the real estate business.

Now we were living the American Dream. We had two mortgages.

Just as the first payment was due, just as we started getting nervous, just as we considered that we might have made a huge miscalculation and overpaid our day laborers, someone bought the home. We each made about $10,000 on the deal, which disappointed us. I mean, Punch made $80,000. That could have been us! Oh, the deceptive lure of easy money.

We just needed to find the right home to flip, that's all.

So, we looked for another home to flip, but noticed the market slipping just a bit. That's when we decided the next home to flip would be the one we were living in. We paid $300,000 for it and asked $550,000. Someone offered us $25,000 less than what it was listed for and we were insulted. *Don't treat us like we treat those guys we hire outside of Home Depot to lay our sod!* We wanted to make a killing.

It's not like we needed to sell our home, but the papers kept printing articles about people selling their homes in California and paying cash for homes in other states like Texas, many of whom moved to the

Lone Star State and are now stranded there with the Dallas Cowboys. There were reality TV programs about flipping homes. It looked like easy money on TV. Punch made some easy money, so we even had a flesh and blood example. The stories just kept coming. We didn't want to leave California. We just wanted in on the Real Estate Fun Park. It was a revival of the 1950s, which in hindsight is only good news for white people.

Then the market dropped a bit more and the next offer came in at $50,000 less than the asking price. Okay, reality was starting to settle in a little. But very slowly.

After three months, we sold our third home and cleared $100,000, which was $100,000 less than our goal. Our initial plan was to use some of the money to restore the old Victorian home we bought, use some as a down payment and put some away. This was a good plan. Now, we had some choices to make. Our Christian real estate agent (who's no longer in the real estate business, by the way) counseled us to consider an adjustable rate mortgage because she assured us that we could refinance our home in three years to a 30-year fixed. *What's the worry? Prices have leveled off, but they'll come back up.* The blind leading the blind seems too innocent. Maybe we all had our eyes closed because we were afraid if the market dropped any more we'd see its underwear.

In our case, flipping our home became a financial pattern and we believed things were okay. We thought this was a normal way to live. I mean, it was a way out of debt. We'd buy a home and within two years acquire enough debt to say, "Well, I guess it's time to sell the house... again." Four homes in ten years during the housing boom. Any idiot who held onto his or her money made a killing. Not us. We bought an old Victorian that needed a kitchen restoration.

Wow.

We have a nice kitchen.

The thing that's ironic about this whole fiasco is that the loan we currently have is now impossible to get. You can't get an ARM loan with a stated income these days. Somehow banks didn't see this as a bad idea from the very beginning. But the thing that is most difficult to deal with is neglecting the truth that all of us know: If it sounds too good to be true, there's a real estate agent involved.

My brother-in-law, Paul, is a multimillionaire who always gives us good financial advice. In my gut, I knew before we signed on for this loan that I should call him. He is a savvy business executive. Thus the multimillionaire thing. I thought of calling him several times, but then my wife and I started talking about how much it will cost to renovate the historic home we wanted to buy. With an adjustable rate mortgage, we could buy the home for no money down, just like in those late-night commercials, which when they were running I remember someone telling me, "It's impossible to buy a home with no money down." We were witnessing a miracle. And because of it we could use the cash to restore the Victorian home to its former glory. I hate to say we were fools, but we were fools. *Who believes commercials?*

As Christians, where was the Gospel to inform our views on these matters? The culture swept us along. Once you find your own judgmental self in the same type of situation, which I did, suddenly you have a lot more empathy for others. God doesn't treat us as our sins deserve, but that doesn't mean we might not lose our home. God tells us why he takes our money away from us sometimes: "Why should a fool have money in his hand to buy wisdom when he has no sense?"[3]

It's a painful truth because, unlike most parents, God is not permissive. Like the wise parent that he is, he might allow the consequences of our actions to be our discipline. He doesn't pamper us. He disciplines us so that we may share in his holiness, not in the American Dream.

The misfortune of others looks a lot different to me these days.

There but for the grace of God... goes my home loan.

The reality of our financial situation was about to hit us.

Hard.

Right in the middle of Starbucks.

---

3 Proverbs 17:16

YOUR CARD
HAS BEEN DECLINED
(Pefects Moments for a Spit-take)

✦✦✦✦✦✦✦✦✦✦✦✦✦

You know you're in the middle of going broke when you're no longer welcome at Starbucks. That's how going broke works. I walked into Starbucks, ordered an iced chai tea, handed the barista my debit card and took a big sip of my chai tea while waiting for my card to clear, which it didn't. So there I am with a mouth full of iced chai tea that's not even mine. How do you handle this situation? Do you spit it back in the cup? Do you swallow and pay for what you drank? Here's a good rule of thumb: don't take a big swill of your drink until it's paid for, this way when they tell you that your card's been declined you can avoid the spit-take.

"It's been declined."

Liquid spews from my mouth in surprise.

You don't want to be staring at your friendly neighborhood Starbucks' barista, chai tea dripping down her face and no cash in your wallet. Note: Always tip people you spit on.

Thus began my financial awakening.

Eventually, the tension of our checkbook caught up with us. Some people refer to this tension as reality, but let's not mince words. Reality hit again when Apple computers denied my credit card even faster than Starbucks, in less than 30 seconds. I'm typing this on my 2004 PowerBook with the crack that causes goop to gel around my screen on the inside. I only have ¾ of a screen to work on. That's the reality of it.

"How will you write a book on a laptop with only ¾ of a screen?"

Shorter sentences.

Most of us have experienced the embarrassing situation of credit card denial. And if you haven't, I guess you're reading this just to feel better about yourself.

Congratulations! You're not me.

Usually, it goes down like this.

As the cashier at Target is scanning my items, I make small talk.

"How about that?"

"You ain't kiddin'."

Things along those lines.

Then: "Your card has been declined."

REJECTION.

The established financial world has rejected me, but they are still thankful for my business. They want me in debt. Forever. You, too. My self-esteem plummets, because in real life self-esteem is tied to the Dow Jones Industrial Average, which is how credit card companies (also called "banks") have arranged things. This way, I will strive to be accepted by them again someday. You are not a true American without plastic money.

By telling me my card has been declined, Target has called my patriotism into question. I have a Target Visa, and my face turns as red as the card after she tells me. I blend in with the Target logo on the wall behind me and slink out of the store, a headless shopper.

You will want to hide your financial troubles from everyone, like we do when people invite us out to lunch after church and I say, "Sorry, it's not in the budget."

As if we even *have* a budget.

Facing reality helps. Putting up a front never does. Besides, your "best face forward" facade will always be found out. You can fool some of the people some of the time, but never the waitress at Applebee's.

"Your card was declined, Sir."

"Well, that's a shame, because your food was eaten."

I've known for the last three years that if we didn't change things we'd end up living an insecure-paycheck-to-paycheck-hope-we-can-keep-our-home existence, which we did. What good's a home if it's filled with insecurity, anger, resentment, and bitterness? Not that I don't enjoy my mother-in-law's visits. I'm just saying.

If you recognize yourself in any of the above scenarios or find yourself in a situation like ours, then be encouraged that there are other people in the world who use powdered milk. Welcome to the club.

The most important thing I learned from this whole fiasco is that our hearts, not our bank accounts, determine our financial well-being. That's one reason it's so hard to examine our finances – they tell us so much about our hearts. My wife and I were in a mess because of deeply ingrained attitudes and assumptions, like thinking my dad would write me a check to bail us out. He's been dead since I was eleven, so you can see how deeply this was ingrained. But we cannot improve our situation if we don't look at what our heart is financing.

I wanted to take it further than behavior modification, and look at the gospel and how our money managing either testifies that we get the gospel or we don't. And by "get it" I mean understand and embrace and submit to Christ as God in the flesh who died on the cross in our place (justification), satisfied the wrath of God by doing so (propitiation) and rose again three days later that we might live new lives because God has given us new hearts (regeneration). You know? Get it. If we get it, our money managing habits will change. By repentance or the discipline of God's hand. I'd suggest repentance, being a recipient of the latter.

Otherwise, we will continue to fall prey to the god of consumption and the liturgy of the mall. James A.K. Smith, in his book, *Desiring the Kingdom,* has a thesis about secular religious practices, what are often called liturgies. Liturgies are habit forming practices that shape who we are as we participate in them. They show us things we love and the things we love define us. The mall has a liturgy. It promotes a kingdom of consumption, implying that you will flourish better if you have these things. Marketing is its evangelism. It's gospel tells us that something is broken. See all the beautiful people in the ads. You are not like them. This tells you something is not right with you. Their answer is that you need the goods and/or services they sell to be the person you want to be. This outfit, that hair product, this, that or the other thing. The mall presents a liturgy that is formative in shaping our identity. It reflects a certain view of what the good life is all about. And our culture says the good life is about having the next new thing. Materialism isn't about greed. It's about people trying to save themselves through consumption.

Truth be told (which is where the true gospel starts), I don't think I ever had a rock solid determination to get out of debt. I didn't want to escape creditors as much as I wanted to escape the depression that our financial meltdown brought. I said to myself (probably on the advice of a wealthy financial guru who wasn't experiencing depression), "I'll do anything that doesn't violate God's will to get out of debt!"

What exactly did I have to do?

How humiliating will it get?

Well, it all started with the Census Bureau.

4

KEEPING YOUR PART-TIME JOB A SECRET
(So It Won't Ruin Your Career)

••••••••••••

"A census taker once tried to test me.
I ate his liver with some fava beans and a nice Chianti."

— HANNIBAL LECTER,
A FICTIONAL CHARACTER WHO EATS FICTIONAL PEOPLE

It should be clear by now that my wife and I haven't been good financial planners. Our initial plan was to home school our kids and charge 'em tuition. Apparently, there's some sort of state regulation against this. But we still homeschool. The financial upside is obvious. This way, when their lunch money is stolen... it stays in the family.

This book was my second plan. My plan was to write a humor book about getting out of debt and then use the advance from the publisher to get out of debt. After just a few pages into it, this plan didn't seem like a sound one either, since I haven't finished the book yet. This is all I have so far. Unless they want to publish a really short book:

My wife and I spent all our money, then this nice publisher gave us an advance and now we're good. You should write a book. Thanks for reading. Hope that helped.

I want to get out of debt. That is my dramatic need. If this was a screenplay, that would be my goal, which is why this isn't a screenplay. Watching someone bite his nails while shuffling through bills is not really the cinematic experience most people want. Maybe I'll write a screenplay about a comedian who follows the advice of a famous financial guru to get out of debt, then writes a humor book about following this guru's advice to get out of debt and just as the book is starting to sell, the comedian is sued by the financial guru for copyright infringement and the comedian has to go back into debt to hire a lawyer. That would be a funny story.

Regardless, it's time to take action, just like in the movies.

There has to be some way that we can earn some extra cash. I think my wife can get by with one kidney. That's right. Harvesting organs and selling them on the black market can supply our family with a second income. That's a creative idea.

Lemme ask my wife.

I'll be right back.

ᖗ

Yeah, that wasn't well received.

"Why not your kidney?" she said to me.

So, at least she's open to the idea of selling a kidney. I just think it's a better sell to say, "This kidney belonged to a drop-dead gorgeous blond."

Once you go broke, you begin looking for a way out. You might find yourself going through your bills and thinking, "Man, there is no way I can get out of debt – unless my spouse dies." Not that you would wish that, but you're just sitting there, making out checks. "Hey, honey, how you feeling? Just thinking 'bout ya. Doing the bills and thinking 'bout ya. I've done the math and you gotta go. I can't keep you."

I could get a job at Starbucks. But then I'd have to work 40 hours a week and bring home maybe $300. That's no good. Besides, if I was at Starbucks right now blending your Frappuccino I wouldn't have time to write about not working there. Maybe there is another way.

What about selling our home?

We might be able to sell our home and make a profit, but I don't want to consider that yet. I like our home. We bought an old Victorian from 1898 and restored it. Victorians hold their market value better than subdivision homes because they're a specialty item. Of all the homes we've ever lived in, we love this one the most. Selling it is not something I want to think about right now.

What about harvesting organs?

Shot down again.

"What about a second job?" asked my wife.

"Who'll watch the kids?"

"I meant for you," she said.

A second job?

If you take the idea that one of the roles of the man in marriage is to provide for his family, you begin asking God questions. "Lord, I could quit being a comedian and do something else, but what else? What am I qualified to do?" I don't know what I'd do if I didn't do standup comedy. Become a preacher? Most comedians are just preachers who haven't answered their call. Look at Chris Rock. He's preaching. It's just a different gospel. Anyway, it's too late to turn back now. What kind of job could I even get? I don't have a plan B. I do have an idea of what kind of career I could end up in and that's the scary thing. "Hey, does anybody feel like pizza? I've got some pull with Dominoes now."

If I just quit without a plan, wouldn't that be presumptuous? "Please, Lord, make my path straight. And balance my checkbook." Okay, that last line wasn't part of the prayer, but you get the idea.

That's when the screen went black and the title of this movie appeared: *The Census Worker*. It's about a man who decided to apply for a temporary position with the U.S. Census Bureau to help pay down his debt. Based on a true story.

Uncle Sam wants me.

I think that phrase was a compliment at one time.

That's right. To avoid financial ruin I became a government worker, which is kind of like taking a vow of silence to improve your marriage.

The first step was a written test, which was filled with story problems that made me feel even more depressed, because, well, they're story problems. I was so depressed that I was relieved when they hire me. When you *want* to work for the government, you know you've hit rock bottom.

I want Uncle Sam.

It was a low point.

So, I walk into the first day of training at the U.S. Census Bureau, which is basically a room of other depressed and hopeless people (mostly real-estate agents) filling out paperwork. Honestly, I almost leave and never come back. Why? Because it feels completely humiliating. I'm certainly not famous, but when my family and I go to Disneyland (we have season passes) once in a while strangers approach me and ask me if I'm Thor Ramsey, which I am.

But I wouldn't be at the Census Bureau.

"Are you Thor Ramsey?"

"I do not know the man."

"You're not a comedian?"

I would have denied myself three times.

All the fears of what people will think come screaming into my mind: "If word gets out that I've taken a part-time job, people will think my comedy career is sputtering, about to take a nose-dive. I'll be perceived as being dead in the water. Getting out of debt could hurt my career."

That's just a sample of what runs through my head. The only comforting thought I have at the time is, "Well, at least I'm not a real-estate agent."

Then I think of my family, my responsibility to provide, to get us out of debt. I'll have nothing to provide my kids with if we don't get out of debt, that's for sure. So, I stay, raise my right hand and am sworn in as an official government employee, taking the same oath of office as representatives of Congress.

When I arrive home with an arm full of papers the Census Bureau gave me, my wife asks, "What's all that?"

I say, "I can't tell you because I work for the government now."

"Should I expect a scandal?"

"Well, I did take the same oath as a Congressman."

Sworn to an oath of secrecy, because this census stuff is very touchy stuff. Do you want a group of strangers knowing how many people live in your home and what race they are?

The Census Bureau is big on race. They have oodles of choices for race. You know, like Indian from India, Indian *not* from India, Indian from Indiana. And multiple choices under the heading Hispanic, which they don't allow as a category itself anymore.

But they have only one category for the white people – *white*.

First, it doesn't reflect reality. There is more than one kind of White. They could have offered Lily White – for people who play badminton and have nicknames like Bunny and Muffy.

White Trash – for people who can drive their homes and have nicknames like Scooter and Bill (I can't pay the bill) Bill.

Pink – for elderly white people.

Obama White – for white people who want to hide it.

Then there's Bryant Gumbel White.

White Supremacists – ironically, these are the white people with the lowest self-esteem.

And finally – Republican.

So, it was my part-time job to count people of all races, red and yellow, black and white. Please choose one.

The census doesn't monitor religious affiliation. However, here's something interesting I learned during the training classes. As a census worker, I can't dispute what you say. If I ask some guy what race he is and he says, "Cow," then I can't argue with him about it. I just mark the box and move onto the next question about how many teats he has.

The training itself was at points incredibly boring in a way that only the government can make something incredibly boring. The government seems to have standards of boring. Every document must be approved by the Committee for Boring Language Choices before it can become an official U.S. training manual. Even the term government worker makes you feel insignificant. Government worker, worker ant. Whatever. Just waiting for someone to douse our training class with a garden hose.

The first day is the most humiliating.

This is what my life has come to – government worker? Wait. That's not true. *Part-time* government worker.

Then my mind calms down a bit. The location I'll be working from is another city, not the city I live in, which eliminates the fear of knocking on the door of someone I know.

"Hey, how's that comedy thing going?"

"Shut up, Cow Man."

Then the fear of being recognized surfaces again.

One weekend out of town, doing my main gig as a *full-time* comedian, my ride to the event picks me up at the airport and during the drive says to me, "I looked you up on the web. I didn't realize you were famous."

"Well," I said, "if someone doesn't realize you're famous, then you're not famous. But thank you."

The thing I find comforting about Los Angeles is that it's full of famous people I've never heard of, like all of those contestants on *Dancing with the Stars*. I've never even heard of half of them, but they're *stars*. Fame is a very relative thing.

This lady who sits in front of me at the census training keeps saying, "You look really familiar."

She says it three days in a row.

I just give her a matter-of-fact, "Hmmm."

But I think the humiliation of taking on another job is common among us humans. Who knows? Many of the people in the training class may feel the same way I do. They might all be saying to themselves, "I hope no one recognizes him."

I believe that's how many of us get into these situations to begin with – we're concerned about what other people think. That's why we have a good job (or did) and a nice home and two cars and 2.8 well-groomed children. *That third kid doesn't bathe as often.*

But we must face the reality of our own facade.

The truth is this job helped pay down my pride more than anything.

That's when the lady who kept asking me who I was says, "I have to leave early today. I have rehearsal tonight."

"Oh," I said, "Are you in a play?"

"No," she said. "I'm on *Dancing with the Stars.*"[4]

---

4 Comedic embellishment.

5

STAYING MARRIED
WHEN YOU'RE BROKE
(Because It's Cheaper Than a Lawyer)

◆◆◆◆◆◆◆◆◆◆◆◆◆

Along with traveling to perform on the weekends, the part-time job during the week and climbing out of this financial hole, we are trying to stay married, which we've found much easier to do since we're broke. We can't afford a divorce. Blessing in disguise. Our marriage isn't in jeopardy, just our checkbook. I would never leave my wife for the simple reason that if I leave her, *then* who would I blame for our financial crisis?

When you go broke, you will want to blame someone. My wife is used to it. But I can't blame my wife, because, well, I married her. She can't blame me, because, well, it's not my fault. C'mon now! She handled the checkbook, which worked out great... for the economy.

The bottom line is that my wife and I are broke. We did not plan well. We spent all our money on Starbucks. I guess. That's who I can blame! Starbucks! *Man, that coffee's good. Here's all our money!* That might sound stupid to you, but what have you got to show for your money?

At least I'm awake.

As it turns out, being broke also keeps you up at night.

Who knew?

When my wife and I were dating, she had a great paying job, a new car, and a jet ski. We always assume people with lots of toys are good with money. How else could they afford all those toys? I was just thankful that I found a woman who would keep my finances in line. You know, take care of me.

My dad died when I was eleven and being raised by a single mother subconsciously taught me a lesson that many boys learn: Women take care of men. Not just tenderly, the way they baby you when you're sick because you're such a big baby when you're sick, but in every way, both financially and emotionally. So, like many boys raised by a single mother, I grew up to be an irresponsible young man who dated women who took care of me. Sometimes I had to date more than one at a time so they could get the job done. I was a handful.

Now, this isn't to disparage single mothers who are doing the best they can as mothers who are trying to fulfill the role of the absent men in their lives, too. It's to disparage the 40 percent of men who are getting these women pregnant and then not taking any responsibility.

For the longest time, I had difficulty relating to men. I didn't hunt or fish or watch sports or work on cars. And "Hey, did you guys watch *What Not to Wear*?" doesn't cut it as a conversation starter with men. I was like so many men today. Too many men today are just like women except for the fact that they are men. You may be told that gender distinctions don't matter, but you will find that they do, especially if you've ever got your zipper caught. Now, I don't want to do a disservice to sensitive males by making them think that being a man is about their hobbies rather than their character. You shot a deer in the woods. I shot a comedy special in Detroit. We can both be men.

When my wife married me, I was a man who didn't talk about money and felt okay with a woman supporting me. What a catch! I was not taking responsibility. I was depending on my wife the way I had depended upon my mom.

One of the clues to our bleak financial future was how I handled money when I was single. As a single man I found myself reasoning like this: I would open up a bill, look at my checkbook and say, "I can make it up next month." The second month would come and I would say, "I can make it up next month." When the third month came, I just said, "Well, I ruined my credit now, so... why even pay for the junk ('dung' in the King James)?"

If I can't pay my bills, maybe I can at least avoid responsibility.

Then I married my wife and gave her my checkbook. Eventually. After the day she called me up on my cell phone and said, "Yeah, I just wanted you to know I can't call you from home because the phone's been disconnected."

"Hmmm. They disconnected our phone?"

Hmmm, I was very surprised. I was amazed that they would shut off *our* phone. I mean, we have the money to pay them. It's in the bank. So what could it be? It sounds like a conspiracy to me. I mean, is it personal? They just don't like me?

"Honey, I don't understand. Why they would shut off our phone?"

My wife said, "Well, let me explain it to you, Peach. The money that we have in our bank. They want it in their bank. And when YOU don't send them OUR money from OUR bank, THEY shut off the phone."

"All of 'em?"

"Yeah, all of them."

I thought maybe they might just punish us. Shut off a few phones. You know, shut off the phones downstairs. Make us run upstairs to answer.

There is no other way to put it. I was an idiot when it came to handling money. Shoot. I believed commercials where they offered "90 days same as cash," which doesn't really work out that way. Pull three pages from your calendar and then go to your local bank and try to exchange them for cash. You can even show them the advertisement that proclaims "90 days same as cash" and they still won't give you any money.

I make a good living. Yet, I have managed to save zero. Well, that's not accurate. I *have* managed to save zero. So, I did accomplish that. My wife matched my savings and we combined them, but even that didn't seem to help.

My burden isn't debt.

It's regret.

This is where the bitterness comes in: My wife was in the corporate world before she became a stay-at-home mom. The temptation when you're struggling financially is to have her become a stay-at-work mom. When she worked in the corporate world she was responsible for more than 70 people. She was accustomed to lots responsibility, so when she became a stay-at-home mom she took over the finances. Being a standup comic, I was used to avoiding responsibility. There's something comforting about being the breadwinner and not having to worry about the bread.

My wife: "Honey, we're short this month."

Me: "Hey, I don't keep the books."

Honestly, I was more than happy that she was responsible for all the bills because I've avoided responsibility my entire life. That's what comedians do. We make jokes. We don't face reality. Though, I did make some suggestions, which allowed me to do nothing but shift the blame. You see the genius of my plan?

Do I blame my wife that we're broke?

Yes. Of course.

What else am I going to do?

Take responsibility?

That's what makes it so comical. I blamed her for decisions that I never followed through on. It's like when a guy gets mad at his wife because he can't find something around the house. Somehow men think that women should know where everything in the house is at any given moment.

How should we deal with the bitterness?

I'll tell you as soon as I find my notes.

"Honey, what did you do with my notes? Oh, that woman!"

There are no fancy tricks to getting out of debt. Unfortunately, there is no lap-band for your wallet. I'm just amazed that my wife and I can talk even about our finances. Sometimes. It's like running that potato sack race at the county fair. If you didn't happen to grow up in rural Nebraska, don't worry, I'm sure you've seen potato sack races in movies. The point is both of you have one leg in a bag and you have to run together. Now, it doesn't help that you're being chased by a Financial Beast of a dog, but you can only do it together. You'll have to talk about money together.

Not yell.

My biggest breakthrough in taking responsibility happened when my wife spoke to her multimillionaire brother about our financial situation. My brother-in-law designed some kind of computer chip, started a company in Silicon Valley and sold it. Now he just works to keep from being bored. He's a caring brother who offered her $8,000 to keep us afloat. I felt utter humiliation, which is just a notch above complete humiliation. My wife was just looking for a way to help our family. Not that it wasn't a kind gesture, but borrowing money from relatives will only insure that one of you never shows up for Thanksgiving dinner again.

Boy, did I want to take that money. But saying no was a first step in taking responsibility.

At some point, you have to admit: It's your fault.

That's right. You're to blame for my financial woes. Now, what are you going to do about it? *Casting blame knows no bounds.* But if it were not for late notices, I would not have known sin.

In a marriage there is only one way to take responsibility and that is together. There's only potato sack in this race. Supporting one another spiritually and emotionally is vital, because things are going to get bleak.

So, you can't go blaming each other for your bad money habits.

That's what parents are for.

6

RICH DAD
(And Other Men My Mother Never Married)

My parents never talked about money. They screamed about money. They nagged about money, but they never talked about money. Nagging about money is just as bad as fighting about money. It really has the same effect on the kids, who say to themselves: "Man, I'm never going to talk about money with anyone because all you do is fight about it. I'll just deny it exists."

That kid would be me.

Some of our money habits were learned from our families, which is what makes personal finances *personal*. When two people join in holy matrimony they bring a collective financial history with them. Well, in our case collective is the wrong word. The only thing we collect is debt. In this respect, my wife and I have always been a perfect match: We both believe in spending money. *Until debt do us part.*

One of my earliest memories of moola is about a special lunch program that my mother wanted me to join. It was third grade and my father was having heart problems, so finances were as short as my pop's breath. Mom wanted to sign me up for some program where I could get free lunches. But to get the free lunch you had to line up with all the other kids who received free lunches, like the freakishly tall and skinny kid whose pants buttoned at his chest while his pant legs just cleared his knees. I still have their photos. Hey, wait a second. That's me!

This was rural Nebraska potato-sack-racing land, so it was only about six or seven kids but it was six or seven kids I didn't want to eat lunch with, because wherever you stood in line is where you had to sit at the lunch table. Taking my mother up on her policy of "you can tell me anything," I told her that I didn't want to get free lunches and I told her why – I might get the cooties. I was embarrassed by the idea of getting a handout. But with his heart condition, my dad's income had suffered because he couldn't work the same hours, which according to mom were "more hours than there are in a day." That's a lot of overtime. Mom told me that I didn't have to take the free lunches.

Even after the free lunch crisis, I still never had the impression we were poor. I was sheltered from the shame of being one of the free lunch kids who all dressed like they were poor and were unpopular with the other kids. No one has to know you're poor if you spend all your money on the right clothes. It's something we all understand about money from a young age: Money is about image. Keep a good one. That's the first money lesson I learned well. I always had nice clothes. Who says you can't sleep in a thousand dollar suit... out on the curb... next to the dumpster?

When I was a kid, every day before school my mother would give me "milk money," which was money that I used to buy candy with after school. Got milk? No, I got candy! It was money budgeted for milk, but I spent it on candy. That's the second money lesson I learned well. Don't use your money for what it's intended, use it for something that tastes good, like the Dish NFL package.

However, it was the homemade bike that did me in.

All the other kids in my neighborhood were peddling around on Schwinn Apple Krates and Orange Krates, the popular brand name bikes of the day. I think they all had brand name bikes. It's hard to tell when you're riding your bike around with a paper bag over your head.

The Apple Krate bike was a flamboyant red (the official name of the color) and came with a shy and reserved banana seat, a five speed Stik-Shift, a MAG sprocket (I prefer Spacely's), stingray handle bars, and a front tire that was small like on a chopper motorcycle. They were the coolest bikes around. So, naturally, I didn't have one.

The Apple Krate kids would park their bikes in a row at the baseball park, a display of what the rest of us didn't have – rides to the game. I remember clearly they were Schwinn bicycles, because they had logos. This logo meant "cool." Those kids with bikes from Sears couldn't compete. We were kids, but we knew the score. Logos mean something. Schwinn stood for quality while Sears stood for cheap. My homemade bike stood for "my dad grew up during the depression."

Depression era bikes do not have logos.

While all my friends showed off their new bikes, mine was made by my father, who loved to create mechanical oddities like lamps made out of driftwood so we could swim at night and coffee tables made out of wagon wheels that would rotate the dip. So, when I asked for a new bike, he informed me that he would build me one. He spent as much money on the new seat and handle bars and tires and peddles as he would have spent on a new bike. But it wasn't new. It was a spray painted old frame with new parts. It was unique, I'll give it that. How many bikes have a chip dip holder? I just wanted a bike like everyone else. A bike with a logo.

Homemade bikes have no logos.

And there was no spray paint with sparkles in it for the consumer, so my bike had a dull matte finish.

I was determined that things would be different when I got older.

When I became an adult, I wanted everything to be new and brand name. It took years to appreciate the quaintness of vintage. Not that I want our vintage to actually be vintage. I'd rather pay for something brand new that was made to look vintage. Initially, our search for "vintage" looking kitchen cabinets began at Home Depot. Then we had "an appointment" with a kitchen designer who wasn't part of a warehouse chain store. She was with a "specialty" store. You see? We wanted our kitchen to be special. And it is. Three times as special as a Home Depot kitchen. People walk in and "oh and ah" and can't find the fridge because it looks like part of the cabinetry. That's worth three times the special.

To this day, I've never bought anything off of Craig's List, America's Internet garage sale. My wife buys 'stuff' ('dung' in the King James) from Craig's List all the time. Before our second child, when the money was flowing and the economy was booming, I would always say, "I'm not gonna have my kid playin' with that secondhand stuff." Then I'd go out and buy a new Playskool large plastic house, because toddler real estate prices hadn't gone bust yet. Thanks to Craig's List, kids are flipping Playskool homes.

Our second child's toys are all from Craig's List. Little Kate Tulip is only two-years old, but she'll soon be able to recognize name brands, distinguishing old things from new things. She already knows who Elmo is and she loves him, which makes me feel a little better, because he already looks secondhand.

My wife and I have similar financial backgrounds which means that neither one of us married for money. Her father was a choral music teacher and my pop had his own small trucking company. Now you may assume that my dad could beat up her dad, but her dad taught choral music in Saudi Arabia for over a decade. This makes him the Clint Eastwood of choral directors. "Get off my sand." As a choral music teacher in Saudi Arabia he made the same wages as a doctor in America. Since there is nothing to do in Saudi Arabia but distill your own whiskey and save money, he saved a ton of money. Unfortunately, he can't remember where he hid it all because he distilled his own whiskey. But my wife didn't live with her father growing up, so the only financial lesson she learned from her dad was that to save money you have to leave civilization. Duly noted.

Another thing I remember vividly about money growing up is that my mother didn't like how my dad managed his business. She was always complaining about a customer who owed him money that he wasn't collecting from quick enough. However, to my dad, the people he did business with were his friends, so he'd let them slide. Mom resented this. I think. Maybe she smashed the dishes for other reasons, but this combination taught me to avoid talking about money at all costs because you can't have cookies and milk when all the cups are broken.

Maybe that's why I struggle with talking about the simplest money matters. Like today, I returned some anti-slide coasters for our couch to Home Depot while my wife waited in the car with the kids. Home Depot gave me cash, nearly seven whole dollars. Now, I returned these coasters because they didn't work. Every time you sat on the coach it slid across the wood floor. The mission was to find some anti-slide coasters that do work so we can sit on the couch without needing a travel agent. So, I found some other rubber grip pads to set the couch on that were only four bucks and I used our debit card to pay for them.

Well, I put the seven bucks in my wallet so I can have a guilt-free trip to Starbucks, meaning that my wife won't see it on our online bank account, which tells all. I should probably give up Starbucks altogether, but that's one card I ain't cuttin' up – my Starbuck's gold card. Because now it's on my i-Phone. The gurus just say to cut up all your credit cards. My rule is if you can pay cash for Starbucks you can have some. But daily? I probably spend about $150 a month on Starbucks.

I'm certain I'll tell my wife all of this before she reads it. Show her the advance check the publisher gave me. Buy her a Starbucks. Then tell her. That's a good rule: anytime you have to confess something to your wife, buy her a Starbucks first. Caffeine makes people forgive faster. Right? Speeds things up.

Get her a drink that's swirly.

Do you find yourself doing things like this because you fear it might lead to an argument about money?

Oh, you don't.

Oh.

Awkward silence.

I never felt deprived of anything as a kid, besides a logo for my bike. But I never thought we were rich, either. We did live in a big house, but it was an old house, so it didn't qualify as a rich person's house to me. That's why this whole American Dream is very relative. In grade school, one of the kids commented about "not being rich like you. We don't live in a big old house." To him, rich equaled the size of your home. To me, rich equaled new. After buying our first home, I was disappointed that it didn't come with a logo.

Even though my grandpa was an accountant, I don't think my mother balanced a checkbook until my dad passed away. However, she always championed savings. Not that I had a personal savings account growing up, but I was always told it was a good idea. But there was this underlying philosophy that you had to be rich to save money. We didn't have the extra money rich people had, all our money was sitting uncollected in the wallets of dad's friends.

My wife's mother was originally a member of Hollywood's elite, the daughter of an MGM's prop master who worked on the *Wizard of Oz* among other films while she herself frolicked around the backlot with child actors like Margaret O'Brien, Dean Stanton and Robert Blake. She married into the lower showbiz rung of Saudi Arabian choral music directors, but she never stopped spending money like she was from Hollywood's elite.

That pretty much summed up our view of money. We spent money like we were rich. And to some people, we are rich. This makes our spending habits all the worse.

You can get a glimpse of your financial future by looking at your parents. Now, if that doesn't rattle your financial cage with fright that knocks your change together, nothing will. Do you want that kind of financial future?

I know a young newly married woman who grew up in a financially well-to-do but unstable home. Her father made a lot of money, so they spent a lot of money. And in spending so much, her parents always fought about money. This young woman decided that would not be her future. Thus, she became a financial miser, even resentful of tithing to the point that her husband has to write the checks for church as long as he can find where she hid the checkbook. She can't bring herself to give money away.

The problem with this kind of overcorrection is that it's behavior modification and not heart-driven change. If she doesn't cooperate with God and develop a generous heart, then she will likely propagate the reverse problem in her children. As adults, her children will complain, "My mother was such a miser we couldn't buy anything new. We couldn't buy anything old. So, now we buy whatever we want." That's what can happen when we don't see our finances as an issue of the heart.

Unless we become aware of how our financial past has shaped us, we might be doomed to repeat it or swing the opposite dysfunctional direction. Even now, I have to admit that the name Schwinn doesn't mean the same thing it did to me as a kid. When I was a kid it meant cool. Now it just means I wasn't allowed to have cool things as a kid. What a horribly relative association brand names bring.

Ultimately, we can't really blame our parents for our bad financial decisions. At least not in print. Sure, parents can play a large role in training up their children in wise ways, but children eventually have to decide to walk in those ways. Even if our parents didn't train us wisely, the wisdom is out there if we truly seek it. (See the book of Proverbs.) Many of us think our lives would not only be better if our parents had trained us better, but we think that our lives would be better if our parents were wealthy and gave us a stack of James Madisons.[5]

I know this much, speculation will not get us out of debt.

My wife and I realized that before we could begin any financial turnaround, we both had to want a turnaround. Couples need to agree. If one is moving forward and the other is moving backward, well... do the math... you can't ride a tandem that way. I don't care if it is a Schwinn.

Sit down (fore to aft), agree that you're in a mess, and ask God to change your hearts.

Now, begin pedaling.

---

5 He's on the $5000 dollar bill. Yeah, I've never seen one either.

7

WHO NOT TO PAY
WHEN YOU'RE BROKE
(Otherwise Known as a Budget)

♦♦♦♦♦♦♦♦♦♦♦♦♦♦

This month it looks so bleak that I think it is going to be the first month that we miss our mortgage payment. "Missed a payment" makes it sound like we tossed some money at the bank but overthrew them. "Look, guys, I said down and out, not a slant!" If they ran the right route our money would be... on the money. Since I'm going with the sports analogy, our situation is more like we don't have a football to throw. You can't miss a pass without a football. If we don't get a football soon, they're going to cancel our game.

One good paying gig for the month canceled today, the week before I was to be there. That's the money we budgeted for our mortgage payment. That was our football. I have another gig next week for a friend, which means it's cut-rate. Right, it's a Nerf ball game. Not official. The refs don't recognize it. The gist is that I'm not getting paid my standard honorarium. I have a great event at the end of the month, but it comes at the very end of the month and we are honestly out of money now.

It looks bleak.

We are broke.

This seems like the perfect time to do a family devotional on fasting.

My poor wife is completely down in the dumps. "Maybe we should declare bankruptcy," she said with a tinge of defeat in her voice.

Forfeit the game?

Two of our closest friends declared bankruptcy and, of course, that taught us a great lesson: Sometimes bankruptcy works out. They appear much better off two years later. I'm not encouraging bankruptcy. All I'm saying is that it worked out for them. *Don't look at me. They're the ones encouraging bankruptcy.*

"That's so encouraging, honey," I said.

"How's bankruptcy encouraging?"

"Well, look at it this way. We're broke, not bankrupt. It could be worse."

"Yeah, I guess. By the way, we're tithing a pound of Morton's salt this Sunday."

Now we have to sit down and figure out who not to pay.

Some people call this a budget.

I hate budgets. It's depressing figuring out how much you owe to whom and then figuring out that you don't have enough to pay them all. You get to the point where you have to put a stop-payment on a check so you can have a birthday party for a family member. *Thanks, Honey, it was a great surprise party!* The biggest surprise was that we didn't have enough money to cover the cake. You might think I'm only saying that to make a joke, but it's the sad truth. My wife threw me a birthday party and actually had to do this. That's how bleak our situation got – we were upside down on a birthday cake. (I don't even like pineapple upside down cake, but it seemed the appropriate cake to buy given the circumstances.)

I have what is called an irregular income, but somehow Macy's doesn't care. They want regular payments from my irregular income. Instead of Macy's, we should have applied for a card at an irregular clothing store. So my sleeves aren't the same length. So what? At least they don't expect regular payments.

I'm taking my business to Gimbels.

What's that? They're a fictional store?

Perfect. All I got's fictional money.

This morning we sat down for breakfast, hot waffles and syrup, and decided to document our cash flow, which is especially difficult to do when there is no cash flowing. My suggestion, before you embark upon any plan, pray with your spouse before you start because you'll come to a subject like "tires" and ask your wife, "How much are tires for the car?" And she won't know. But somehow, since she was the one buying tires in the past you feel like she's being evasive because it's about money. So you'll say, "When you want to know something you know it and when you don't want to know you don't."

Then she'll say, "You're calling me a know-it-all."

"No, I'm not. I'm calling you a conditional know-it-all."

And then you'll have an extra bill to get that syrup stain out of your shirt.

But we needed to figure out who to pay.

Like it or not, we had to make a list of everyone we owed. So we listed everything that came to mind. Things like our mortgage payment, car payments, airport parking expenses, credit card payments, student loan payments, electric, gas, water, internet, cell phone bills, health insurance, auto insurance, life insurance, etc. The first thing you'll notice about this list is that we live an incredibly boring life. Who knew it was so expensive to be so boring? I always thought that if I was broke there should be yacht payments and personal coaching fees involved.

Nope.

Gas, water, and fire.

Back in the old days, two of those were free. Today we have to budget for warmth.

Budgeting is hard for us to do because of my irregular income. It's hard to create a budget based on hope.

"We need to make the mortgage payment."

"Well, let's *hope* I get a gig."

To help us figure out our cash flow, I searched online and found some Excel worksheets for budgets. The only problem is that I don't really excel at Excel. I tracked things for four months, but then I stopped because it was depressing. I've doubled up on some payments, but after the interest it's like paying half of what I doubled up on. What? These credit cards are tricky. I bet the guy who owns fire can pay cash.

But it's not just our credit cards, which number twelve. There are two hospital bills, a dental bill, a BillMeLater bill which bills me now and later and a few other stragglers.

It's all there on the sheet.

What isn't on the sheet is the emotional cost of being in debt. Each one of these sheets forges a type of Marley chain of worry and regret that is tethered to my neck. It's like my tie is too tight, which is odd because I don't wear ties. My strides are slower, not bouncy like carefree people who own fire. This is the point when I am most tempted to give up. This is where my wife says something like, "Maybe we should declare bankruptcy." She said this because we are being haunted by debt, the ghost of past due past. Our mortgage is due. I stopped monitoring the sheets after the sixth month. That's not to say we gave up a budget. Here's how I've come to terms with budgets. Budgets are like diets. Some people need Weight Watchers. They need to eat breakfast and then run to the computer to keep tab of their points for the day. And they do this every meal, which is fine. For financially obsessive compulsive people. It works for them. They lose weight.

Other people just decide to eat less. That's all. And they lose weight.

That's how our budget works. We buy less junk. We spend less. We stopped charging things, which is like giving up sugar. We act like the proud Dutch grandparents that my wife descended from and buy cereal that's in plastic bags instead of boxes. Well, we only did that once because I'm not Dutch, I'm German. We're back to boxes now, because all I have to say about cereal in plastic bags is, "Really? This is where you want to cut corners? *I vant my Shredded Mini-Vheats in za box.*"

That's about the gist of it for us – spend less, pay out more until all our debt is gone. Google "frugal." That'll help clarify things.

Honestly, we don't really budget my income. At the moment, we budget my paychecks.

"We have some money. What do we need to spend it on right now? Would you like water and heat?"

"Good choice, honey. Write another check."

"What about health insurance?"

"How much is it again?"

"$700 a month."

"I feel pretty good. How about you?"

At this point our mortgage payment is a luxury item.

This phrase "being upside down on your home loan" really paints a vivid picture, because that's how it feels. It's like our home is trying to flip, the rooftop turning toward the ground, the ground floor reaching for the sky while I'm in the doorway trying to keep it stable, trying to keep it level, trying to maintain it. Everything is out of whack, except my birthday cake, which is the only thing that looks right-side up in this scenario.

At the end of the month, I get a call about doing a commercial for Ashley Furniture HomeStores. On top of that, I get another call for a last minute gig on Saturday. Both of these gigs are sandwiched on either side of my cut-rate gig.

Thank the Lord, we make the mortgage payment.

Barely.

Now, we just have to worry about our car payment.

Again.

8

HAND PAINTED ORANGE VOLVOS
(Who Says New Cars Are a Bad Idea?)
◆◆◆◆◆◆◆◆◆◆◆◆◆◆

My wife and I walked by a BMW convertible and I commented, "That's a cool looking car."

"That's a mid-life crisis car," she said.

"Man, I sure hope I can afford a mid-life crisis."

Cars do say something about how you handle money. The first thing they say is, "You can handle a car payment." This is something to keep in mind when you're dating. If you date someone for more than two months, you can know if they can handle consecutive car payments responsibly. In the third month, if they pick you up in a different car, dump them immediately.

Is it wrong to buy a new car? Is it better to buy a mid-priced used car? How much is that new car smell worth to you? Would you date someone who's car door was held shut by a rope? If you said, "No," to that question then clearly you're not my wife.

It is the common wisdom of financial gurus to discourage people from buying new cars. They always say of new cars, "They are a bad investment." Really? I'm investing in getting to work on time. How about that? It never even occurred to me that I was buying a car to make an investment. It's odd thinking to me. Is a refrigerator an investment? Why not use this same logic when buying home appliances? Buy used because as soon as Sears delivers, you've lost 30% on your investment. Is my food cold? That's why I bought the fridge. I didn't buy it as an investment. And I don't buy cars as investments. Cars are just home appliances you keep outside. I buy a car to drive to work to pay for that fridge to keep my food fresh, so I can have enough energy to get up the next day and do it all again.

When I first ventured into a career in standup comedy, I drove everywhere. Sometimes I would get in the car and drive twenty-four hours to the next comedy club. I put a lot of miles on my car and fast. During a stint in Florida, I stopped by an auto dealership and tried to buy a new car. They wouldn't give me credit because of I was a self-employed standup comedian. My mother lived in Florida, so I asked her to cosign.

My own mother wouldn't give me credit.

Such is the financial reputation of comedians.

So, I've owned my share of clunkers. There is a term to describe people who spend so much money on car repairs that they are suicidal – mechanic depressive. You ever call your car a piece of junk and then end up apologizing to it? Patting the dash, "I'm sorry. You're a good car. Please, please, start – and I'll replace the garbage bag with a real window."

When we first married, my car was such a piece of junk that my wife wouldn't fill it up because she feared the car wouldn't outlast a tank of gas. I'm surprised that our relationship made it through the string of cars I owned. She should have seen the keys to our financial future scratched in the cars I tried to start.

Before I met my wife, my first car was a brand new Chevy Cavalier with four doors. It came with a free crewcut. Who can pass up a deal like that at only 11% interest? I nearly bought a Pinifarina Spider, a two-seater, but at the time I thought I might like to have more than one friend. Now I regret not buying that two-seater sports car. I was young. It was my time to drive like James Dean and not die. Instead, I bought a Chevy Cavalier, which as it turns out is a type of death, socially speaking.

The Chevy dealership gave me a loan because I wasn't a comedian. At the time, I had what many people would consider to be a solid and respectable position as an operations supervisor for a major LTL trucking line. The question they should have asked on the loan application was, "Do you like your job?" Because people who don't like their jobs do a bad job and eventually get canned, which makes car payments difficult. Then I met this girl who liked Chevy Cavaliers and we started dating. So, I had both a job I hated and a relationship I hated.

One was easier to discard than the other.

This was such a bad relationship that I bought this book called *How to Get Away from a Controlling and Overbearing Person*. She found the book. "What's this supposed to mean?" Well, considering that it was hidden under the spare tire in my trunk... I think it means I bought the right book.

Soon after, I met my wife, someone who has always loved cool cars. I'm shocked she even dated someone who owned a Chevy Cavalier. She was driving some sort of Datsun sports car when I met her.

After the trucking company fired me for not liking my job, I started a career in standup comedy and within a year I was working forty-two weeks out of the year traveling around the country doing comedy (at least that's what I called it). I drove that Cavalier into the ground. Or maybe it was the lack of oil that drove it into the ground. Either way, I met my wife because of that car.

I was driving from Des Moines, Iowa, to a one-nighter in Clarksville, Tennessee, when the Cavalier broke down somewhere in the middle of Missouri where they only have enough kids to play six-man football at the local high school and have no need for rental cars. The mechanic was going to have to order a part and it would take a week and all that small town stuff that happens just like in the movies, except that my wife was in another town waiting to be met by me.

I was scheduled to be on the road for three weeks doing comedy. Somehow, I had to make those gigs, because in standup comedy if you don't perform you don't get paid. Being that there was no rental car agency in town, I had someone drive me to the local used car dealership where I purchased a rust colored 1978 Nova for $300, hoping it would get me through the next three weeks. Turns out, it was rust covered. That wasn't paint after all. Initially, I was just hoping to make it to the gig on time that evening. This car situation put me behind schedule, but I had never missed a gig yet. Thankfully, I rocketed into my gig that evening, forty-five minutes late, dashing directly from the car to the stage. The Nova had done its job for the day.

The next evening, I was to perform in Knoxville, Tennessee, just a mere three and one half hours from Clarksville. After my restful Motel 6 night's sleep, the next day I started my journey to Knoxville in my '78 Nova. Approximately twenty-minutes into this journey, the Nova not only looked like a clunker, but it began to sound like a clunker. I say this because there was a sound coming from the engine that went "clunk, clunk, clunk."

Another detour was necessary.

To find a mechanic, I pulled into some type of Quick Shop Seven-Eleven type place to ask around. While standing near my '78 Nova outside the convenience gas mart, I was approached by the entire clan of the Beverly Hillbillies. Clearly, this was before they discovered oil and made it to Hollywood. There was Jed, before he'd lost his weight, and Granny and Jethro and all their earthly possessions attached to the top of their car with a rope. Jed Clampett insisted on having me open the hood so he could take a peek at "the guts," which I was reluctant to do because there was no Ellie May in sight. Just overweight Jed in his overalls, Granny and Jethro as a ten-year old. As Jed tinkered around under the hood, it occurred to me (the young naive chap that I was) that he was trying to finagle a deal. He wanted cash money to fix my car. Initially, I thought who better to fix a '78 Nova than a Hillbilly. Then I noticed that crank on his car and decided to see a mechanic with a sign.

The first mechanic I found told me it was going to be more than the car was worth to fix it. So, I skipped the second mechanic and decided to see how far I could drive the Nova before it gave its last clunk, a kind of how many licks does it take to get to the center of a Tootsie Roll experiment.

It gave its last clunk two miles down interstate 40.

That's equal to three licks.

The Hillbillies waved as they passed me in their model-T.

Now they had Ellie May with them! She must have been inside getting a Slurpee, otherwise I might have given them a chance. But I was destined to meet my wife and neither Ellie May Clampett or a dead Chevy Nova on the side of the interstate could stop me.

Resigning myself to the probability that I would never make this gig on time, I leaned against the Nova and stuck out my thumb. Even in Tennessee, I figured the chances of a hitchhiker with a car getting a ride were slim. But it was only minutes later when a very nice pharmacist in a new car pulled over and offered me a ride all the way to Knoxville. Not only that, about halfway there he insisted on buying me lunch at Cracker Barrel. Being that I was an admitted self-employed standup comedian who was standing next to a broken down '78 Nova, he thought of me as destitute. Junk cars make you feel like junk. This is probably why most of us buy new cars. So, we ate at the Cracker Barrel and to my embarrassment, sat at a table right next to the Clampetts.

When the Pharmacist dropped me off, he gave me his name and number, but since I didn't have a Franklin Planner at the time, I lost it. If you know any nice pharmacists from Knoxville, pass this book onto them. Maybe he'll contact me again one day out of the blue. Anyway, he drove me right to the hotel and that night at the show I met the woman would become my wife.

Three weeks later, I made it back to Missouri and that Cavalier, which I eventually had to abandon in Madison, Wisconsin the next winter. I just left it parked somewhere. The very same day I abandoned my Cavalier, I bought a used Volvo that was hand painted orange with a paint brush. It was $300, which had become my standard price for a car. Once the repair bills for a car exceeded a couple grand, I would just leave the car parked somewhere. The Volvo actually lasted me several months, then it broke down on the side of the interstate outside of Chicago where it remains to this day.

Then the economy turned around and someone gave me a car loan, something I had trouble getting in the past as a self-employed standup comedian. Living in Chicago, I walked four blocks to a local Mazda dealership and they gave me a loan. I didn't even lie on the application. That's how good the economy was at the time. They were just passing out car loans to standup comedians.

I barely qualify to drive a car, let alone have a loan on one.

My wife and I just made our last car payment.

Immediately after paying off this car the temptation was to get a second car because we're a one-car family. My wife has to drive me to the airport and pick me up. I always have to leave before the coffee at Starbucks is even finished brewing and we have two kids who have to get up and ride along. It's very easy to make a second car sound justifiable.

But the car is paid for now.

Click.

The last payment.

Whenever something is paid off online, I think the bank's website should play a little celebration tune for you. But it doesn't. It's just "click" the car's paid for now.

One of our best friends said, "Isn't that a great feeling?'

"No," I said. "It's not. Because we still made a payment. Talk to me next month when we don't have to make a payment. No click. That will be a great feeling."

These days I'm happy to drive a clunker, not that our 2006 Dodge Magnum is a clunker. I'm just happy to drive anything that's paid off. Oddly enough, as soon as a car is paid off it becomes a clunker. The timing of the auto industry is impeccable.

If I had it to do all over again, I would buy that Pinifarina Spider I nearly bought when I was twenty-something. Brand new. Against all the advice of financial gurus everywhere. It was only a two-seater, so I didn't buy it. I guess I expected to have more friends. Turns out, a two-seater would have been perfect. One seat for me and one seat for the friend I wish I had. There are some things you can regret as much as debt.

But I have discovered that clunkers are safer.

While I was out of town, my wife was carjacked in our own driveway. On the bright side, at least she didn't have far to walk home. The car salesperson didn't happen to mention to us that the Dodge Magnum we purchased is one of the top three carjacked cars in the country. We thought we were buying a station wagon, but no. We bought a get-away-car.

The carjackers followed her home from a grocery store. Two of the future inmates ambushed her in the driveway. Initially, the dude holding the handgun asked her for her purse. Then the older dude asked for the car keys. The younger dude asked, "Whatta you doin'?" And the older dude said, "Get in the car," not to my wife but to the younger gang member. The gang member plebe said, "Sorry, Ma'am," to my wife, which I'm sure the judge will take into consideration.

"How do you plead?"

"Guilty. But I said I was sorry."

Then they were gone, followed by the car that dropped them off in front of the house. (I think it was a hand painted orange Volvo.) There were three suspects involved in taking a purse away from a suburban homemaker. It took three men to handle my wife. Maybe they should be looking at people who know her.

For some reason, one of the gang members felt compelled to use my wife's cell phone and call the last person she spoke with, which happened to be me. I was sitting in a movie theater in Nashville, Tennessee, when my phone vibrated. Thankfully, it was such a boring movie (*Australia* with Huge Jackman and Nicole Kidman) that I was looking for any excuse to walkout. So, I took the call, thinking it was my wife because it was her name on the screen.

"Hey, Peach!"

All I hear is cussing on the other end of the line.

"Did I forget to take out the trash before I left?"

This gang member did not take kindly to being called "Peach."

After a few more verbal assaults, he hangs up.

As you can imagine, I am panicked with worry. *He might make a long distance call!* Okay, my real concern was, "Where's my wife?"

She was being interviewed by a local detective who shared many things that frightened her even more – like the one about the carjackers who had recently been taking not only the cars, but the people driving them out to a remote location, shooting the former owners of the autos in the head and then moving on with the car. The detective was just there to help.

The detective asked my wife, "What did they look like?"

She said, "A gun. They looked like a gun." Because when someone is pointing a gun at you, that's what you look at. So, you have to ask yourself, "Is that new car worth it?"

Pay cash for an older car.

It just might save your life.

Unless you're under 25, then buy the sports car.

Brand new.

9

LITTLE THINGS ADD UP
(So Do Big Things, but I Can't Afford Those)

$\bullet\bullet\bullet\bullet\bullet\bullet\bullet\bullet\bullet\bullet\bullet\bullet\bullet$

Starbucks is my happy place, my first romance with corporate America. My local Starbucks' baristas know me by drink. They look at me when I walk in and say, "Venti iced chai? Eight pumps?" This is why I love Starbucks. They always make me feel welcome. I walk in and a barista asks with a big smile, "How are you today?"

"Well, I'm better now that you made me feel welcome."

I don't even care that it's a corporate policy smile. I'll take it. *"Thanks for reading the company manual."* The baristas always put me in a better mood. Just say the word "barista" aloud. It's a very happy word. It's not just iced chai tea. It's iced chai tea and someone who's paid to be glad to see me. That's worth $5.90 a day. (You may have to adjust this joke for inflation.)

Here's my problem: part of the reason I barely have enough to pay my fixed expenses is that I'm spending a lot of money on items that aren't necessities at all. Starbucks is a prime example. You could say Starbucks is one of my greatest weaknesses. Or it's one of my greatest strengths depending upon your view of caffeine.

I have such a love for the place that I'd rather quit paying the utility bill than go without Starbucks. Most of us view heat in our homes as a necessity when that's not the case at all. Heat only makes it easier to sleep. It's not *necessary*. Wouldn't you like to see more babies born? Get rid of heat in your home and your spouse will finally snuggle the way you've always dreamed.

Starbucks is another story. I can live without heat. Starbucks has hot drinks.

The atmosphere is one draw for me. The soothing green color calms jittery coffee drinkers. It invites you back, the warm wood and folksy faux-chalkboard specials and padded chairs and smart-looking people with glasses showing off their Apple products, back when Apple products were something to show off. Plus, the tables are never sticky. They wipe their tables off. That always brings me back.

I'm a gold card member, which is basically a frequent drinking program. My average is $150 a month and with every 12 purchases I get a free drink. *Congratulations.* That's 24 drinks a month, which is two free drinks each month. Minus the savings, I only spend $140 a month at Starbucks. If it wasn't for Starbucks, I wouldn't be saving $10 a month.

But who's counting? Besides the accountants at Starbucks. Yeah, I have a problem and I don't even drink coffee. I drink chai tea and eat pastries, specifically low-fat cinnamon swirl coffee cake. It's low-fat. And it's swirly. Did you hear me? It's swirly.

Don't judge me.

It's swirly.

Besides, I paid cash today with the seven dollars Home Depot gave me from that return.

I'll have to cut back. Cash. Maybe $50 a month. Maybe I can sell something around the house. Maybe we can have a monthly garage sale to supply my Starbucks habit. If it's not in the budget you have to figure out other ways. A lemonade stand maybe? If you sell lemonade to buy Starbucks is that like robbing Peter to pay Paul?

The truth is little things like Starbucks add up. This is not news to you I'm sure. I'll tell you what is news, have a chat with your local Starbucks barista about people's financial habits at Starbucks.

"How many people like myself come in here daily?" I asked my barista.

"Oh, you don't wanna know," she said.

So, there's Starbucks' financial policy – bury your head in the coffee.

"20 or 30?" I said.

"Hundreds."

Some customers come in two or three times a day, she told me. I know. I know. *Their* savings are really adding up. That's like five free drinks each month. These people are saving nearly $25 a month. If I went more than once a day, I could save more money, too. The more you buy, the more you save. That's marketing 101. Wait a second. Marketing is about *getting* my money. Hey! I think I'm catching on.

The crew (now every employee was involved in my financial survey) told me about one customer who orders eight black teas daily. She calls ahead and then comes in and picks up the order, which is $18 (with a $2 tip). That's… carry the one… I don't know… more than I spend there daily. This person is a *really* poor financial planner. If she just drank seven more black teas a day, she could get a free drink every day. Think of the savings.

Little things add up.

If my wife blew $150 this month on various things, which she did because she told me, "I spent $150 on various things at Target today." That means together we blew $300 this month. That's a part-time job at Starbucks. If we just gave up Starbucks it would be like getting a part-time job at Starbucks.

That's $3,600 per year we can save.

Wow.

That doesn't even include the low-fat cinnamon swirl coffee cake, valued at $1,200 per year.

The point is… little things add up.

Big things add up too, but I can't afford them.

Like most Americans, we medicate with money. "Feeling down, Peach? Let's go buy some new lawn furniture for the backyard."

We don't have a drug problem or a drinking problem (aside from Starbucks). We have a shopping problem. Bored? How about some new curtains for the living room? Like any good 12-step program, you have to call upon a Higher Power to help you overcome years of decorative behavior. I mean, destructive behavior.

When you're self-employed you really notice little things like, oh, recessions. When a recession hits, the giving in churches drops even more than usual. When giving drops, there are no extra funds for special events like that workers and leaders appreciation banquet where they bring in a comedian to entertain the group. I'm a special event. So, you notice the money's just not there to spend anymore, which is problematic for people who spend tons money.

"Let's invite some people over for dinner?"

"And feed them what?"

"Oh, I see. You forgot to have the heat shut off."

My wife and I reinforce each other's bad spending habits. No one in our home goes to Target alone. This is why when your spouse begins making good financial decisions you feel threatened. It's like the alcoholic who wants to stop drinking, but his drinking buddy discourages him because he doesn't want to drink alone. That's American culture. No one wants to shop alone. You know you have a problem when you're hiding receipts and returns.

Shopping is a way of life for us. In our minds, we aren't shopping. We are spending quality time together. At Target. The place where we have date night. My wife calls it, "The hundred dollar store," because every time we go we spend no less than $100 on many little things.

"What kind of little things?" you ask.

Forgettable little things.

Toilet paper, cereal, some little toy, a special brand of tortilla chips with specs of olives in them, fruit snacks (which they should make for adults, by the way, because right now I can't breakout the Scooby-Do fruit snacks when the guys come over to watch NFL football), batteries, a combination of necessities and useless-ities.

Eating out several times a week adds up, too. I travel a lot, so when I get home my first thought is always about where we'll eat. It's my way of reconnecting with my family. Things are different when you're broke. Now I eat alone while they wait in the car.

That's a joke.

They wait at home.

Eating out may be a way of reconnecting with my family, not to mention my old friend Pasta Milano, but there must be a way to reconnect that's not so expensive. "Let's try eating at home," I suggested. It was the oddest thing. As a family, we sat down at the dining room table and – no one came to take our order. Dinner time just isn't the same without food and cooks and menus.

Examining our personal financial habits can be discouraging, but I always remind myself, "It's not personal, it's credit."

That's why I now have a library card. My previous habit was to just buy whatever book I wanted at the time. It is always for research. And it's always good to read. We have tax receipts for all the books I bought last year. More than $1500 worth of books. Ironically, I often have to give many of my books to the library to make room on my bookshelf for more books.

Thankfully, now there's Kindle.

The reason most of us start financial plans (and let's be honest, we've all started them… we just fail to finish them) is because we want to change the way we handle money. Then we see how badly we've handled money and grow discouraged. When we are discouraged, we quit.

Then we go to Starbucks to cheer ourselves up.

That's the plan, anyway.

10

IMAGINARY MONEY
(And Other Truths About Credit Cards)
••••••••••••••

My wife had plastic surgery. She cut up our credit cards. *Ba-da-bing.* That's one of the reasons we stopped using them. Because my wife cut them to bits. She cut up the bills, too, but they kept sending us new ones.

Credit cards allow us to fool ourselves. "One pretends to be rich, yet has nothing; another pretends to be poor, yet has great wealth."[6] We can pretend to be rich and yet have nothing. Well, nothing but 14 percent interest. That's something… if you're a loan shark.

Loan sharks are from the olden days before banks took over their business by issuing credit cards. The difference between banks and loan sharks is that loan sharks used to break your legs if you didn't pay. Now, banks just break your credit, so you can't walk financially. To help save us, my wife took scissors to the loan sharks of our lives. She emasculated them. The Apostle Paul would have been proud.

It was a simple but momentous moment. She stood over the trash and snipped them into the recycling bin. Half the card one day, half

---

6 Proverbs 13:7

the next, to put the kibosh on any identity swipers good at jigsaw puzzles.

"How are we gonna buy things now?" I asked.

"There's cash."

"I think I've seen that in movies."

Before she destroyed our cards, we didn't notice our money melting away. Probably because we never really handled our money. I mean, we never really touched it. We had cards. Like most people, I have no problem spending imaginary money.

Imaginary money is credit card money. It's not like we're really spending money. No cash exchanges hands. If banks want to be fooled by this little plastic card, that's their problem. It's imaginary money, which they will soon find out when they try to collect it from me.

"But you charged this!"

"That doesn't mean I had any money. That's why I charged it. Because I don't have any money. If I had money, I wouldn't be charging things."

Silly banks.

When will we learn to stop using credit cards?

Today, I guess. Since my wife cut them up.

Here's an idea I like better than cutting up your credit cards. There is a company that sells a guitar pick punch. It's a handy little gadget that allows you to take something plastic, say like a credit card, and simply insert it, punch it and voilà, it slices your credit card into guitar picks.[7]

We need to find another use for credit cards besides shopping.

James Scurlock writes in his scathing book, *Maxed Out,* "The more people become dependent on credit, the more they need to keep going. Once Americans began using one credit card, for example, they tended to need another. And then another. And then higher credit limits. And then they needed to refinance their homes to pay

---

7 www.pickpunch.com

64

off the credit card bills. And so on. No other product creates that cycle (well, crack and heroin come to mind, but...)"[8]

Thanks to one of my credit card companies, First USA Bank, I discovered just how powerless an individual American citizen truly is when it comes to dealing with the evil of consumer credit.

My story begins as a somewhat innocent (a gracious term to be sure – "blissfully ignorant" would also be accurate or "willfully ignorant" would be right on the money, so to speak) consumer who turns his mailbox key to behold "convenience checks" from First USA Bank. Convenience checks look like regular checks that your local bank sends you, except for the printing at the top that reads, "To Activate these checks call 1-800-whatever."

Not needing the checks, I tossed them in a drawer with other junk mail that I might need one day, like applications for other credit cards.

At the time, I wanted to buy this used digital video camera that was lauded as nearly new. The guy selling the camera by the name of Charles Allen (beware if you know him because he's a shyster) didn't take credit cards and I didn't trust sending him a personal check. Then I remembered those convenience checks. I rushed to my drawer and dug through the credit card applications until I found them. How convenient. They really are convenience checks! I can send the guy a check to pay for the camera, but wait to activate it until I have the camera in my possession. This way I won't get ripped off.

I'm no dummy.

So, I call First USA.

My question is clear: "I received these convenience checks that say, 'Call 1-800-446-1992 to activate these checks!' Does that mean this check isn't good until I activate it?"

"Yes, sir."

"I want to use them to protect myself on a purchase. Can anyone else call this number to activate the check?"

---

8 *Maxed Out* by James Scurlock, page 48

"No, sir."

Thank you and goodbye.

This quick exchange led me to believe that I could sign a check, fill it out, write an amount, but the check still wouldn't be good until I activated it like some sort of check bomb that would explode into money.

It was a 15-second conversation. I didn't get the name of the person I spoke with at First USA, which doesn't matter anyway. Somehow all these individuals morph into one giant collective and evil bank, unless you speak rudely to them in which case they inform you that *they* just work for *them*.

"Well, when you talk to *them* go ahead and pass on what I just said to *you*."

Thinking I was protecting myself, I sent Charles Allen a convenience check for $1,200. Well, interestingly enough, as it turns out, all that is needed to activate the check is my signature. You know, just like a regular check. Something Charles understood because he cashed my check and never sent me the camera. I thought I was protecting myself by using these checks, but all I was doing was exposing my small, small brain.

You may ask, "How stupid can you be?"

Dumb enough to believe a bank.

I'm that dumb.

Banks are determined to manipulate us in any way possible. This is why their language is purposely vague. President Obama signed the Plain Writing Act of 2010 to ensure that the language the Federal Government uses in explaining things to Joe and Jane Public is understandable. It passed in the House of Representatives by a vote of 386 to 33.

The 33 who voted against it are lawyers. I assume.

We've been sold a bill of goods.

The problem with credit cards is that they bill us for the goods we've been sold in the bill of goods that propagates this idea that we need credit cards. Not only are we continually told that we need credit cards, but we're told we need them to live a certain kind of life. World famous film director Martin Scorsese did an American Express commercial where he's picking up photos from his grandson's fifth birthday party and he's unhappy with the narrative thread of the pictures. It's not perfect. He needs to re-shoot, thus he pulls out his American Express card and buys more film. The message is clear — don't hire Martin Scorsese. He can't even keep his grandson's birthday party under budget.

Yet we still think we need plastic to create a life worth living. Credit cards are the communion wafers of the mall's secular liturgy.

Today, we paid off six credit cards. That's good news right? Kind of. Remember? We are the ones handling the accounts. Two of them are one day late. Right. Paying *off* debt and we still can't pay on time. So, we called them and said, "Hey, if you don't charge us this late fee we will pay the entire thing off now." *Do you feel tempted, Big Bank That Wants Us To Keep Making Payments For the Rest of Our Lives?*

They answered: "Good for you. We're still charging you the late fee." In so many words.

I keep hearing stories about how people call their credit card companies and just ask them to lower their interest rates and the banks are like, "Sure. Cool." Does that really happen?

So, the good news is that we paid off six accounts.

The bad news is that we paid off six accounts while incurring extra charges.

Banks are not your friends. They are evil witches who live in ginger bread houses and they will eat you alive. That is their goal. Credit card debt is what a bank uses to capture you and lock you in a cage.

We still have two gigantic cards that triple the debt of these six small ones we just paid off. So, we're not out of the woods just yet. The jubilation is short lived. I keep thinking about all the money we had in the bank before we paid these bills off. It's a wonderful feeling to have money in the bank. Life feels more secure. Until we "click" six payoffs to these banks. Now that money is gone. Life is back to normal. I can't wait to be out from under the evil spell of these last two cards.

11

THE GREAT DEPRESSION
(How It Feels to be Broke)
◆◆◆◆◆◆◆◆◆◆◆◆◆

Depression makes you want to give up.
That's why this book is so short.

I was depressed when I wrote it.

Financially related depression (being broke) is just the opposite of the blanket that makes Harry Potter invisible. With depression, this big wet blanket covers you but it's invisible to everyone else. People can still see you, but not the blanket covering you. You feel alone, you and your invisible wet blanket against the world.

You move slower.

You think slower.

Everything slows down, except the phone calls from creditors.

So, how do you get through it?

I suggest drugs and alcohol. At least that way you have a great excuse for your financial ruin. People will whisper things like, "That poor guy lost everything because of drugs and alcohol."

Unfortunately, I was sober when I made my poor financial decisions. People whisper things like, "That poor guy lost everything because he's an idiot."

I've made my living as a standup comedian for more than twenty years now. Whenever I contemplate my career (which I'm always hesitant to call it because it's more like having friends over, sitting around the living room and talking to them – except you have a mic) I'm always amazed and thankful that I've been able to support my family. All because of jokes. It's a rewarding feeling.

Most of the time.

These days having a nontraditional career means that the money doesn't traditionally flow into our lives the way it did a year or two ago. With things like scripts and books, you do a lot of work *before* you get paid, so the money doesn't flow at all. But if you want to be a writer, there's no other way to go about it.

I want to be a writer.

There's a saying about writing by the author Derrick Jensen: "Writing is really very easy. Tap a vein and bleed onto the page. Everything else is just technical." That's how it's been with this book. Initially, I thought it was a good idea and my literary agent confirmed his belief in this concept, but the more time I spent on this project the more depressing it became for me personally. It's a shock to the system to see how shaped we've been by the liturgy of consumption. But we were fortunate enough to get a book deal, which isn't always the case. Sometimes the greatest pain comes before you even get the deal.

I'm sure you know the feeling. You desperately need money and along comes a deal, an offer, a proposal, a plan that sounds like it could change your financial situation. So, you put everything into it, every fiber of your being and whatever multigrain cereals you can get your hands on. Whatever will help you close this deal. You commit. You steam forward full ahead.

While my literary agent is peddling my goods, other project proposals, a publishing house likes the tone of my writing and they want to consider me for a book idea they have about the Seven Deadly Sins[9],

---

9 Pride (Prov. 16:18); Greed/Covetousness (Eph. 4:19); Lust (Matt. 5:28); Anger (Prov. 15:1); Gluttony (Prov. 23:21); Envy (1 Pet. 2:1-2); Sloth (Prov. 15:19).

of which overspending is not even mentioned. They want one book per sin. This is very good news (as far as news about sin goes). We have a seven book deal on the table. I'm delighted at the thought. It would bolster my writing career, and the advance from the deal is large enough that in one lump sum we would get out of debt. All we have to do now is sit and deliver. (I write in a chair.)

However, the acquisitions editor at the publishing house lets us know that not everyone on the acquisition's team thinks I can pull it off. "He's a comedian. Not a theologian." There is a drawback to having a background in standup comedy, which is that people generally don't take comedians seriously.

The publisher doesn't want a humor book on the Seven Deadly Sins. They want something serious but whimsical in tone. They don't want jokes every paragraph, but being humorous now and then wouldn't hurt. No problem. I can be less funny. That's the easiest part of comedy, being less funny.

Let's get to it.

I research and write and then research and write some more while trying not to dream about how a seven book deal could establish this writing career I'm really hoping will develop. Plus, the advance on this deal could get us out of debt completely. Don't think about it.

For the next month, I research and pound out 20,000 words (four chapters) for the first book in the tentatively titled series *The Seven Deadly Sins (To Name Just a Few)*. I think it's a pretty catchy title. For a book on sin, anyway. In the sample chapters, I cover the story of the seven deadly sins, give a cultural commentary on the sin of pride, expound on the history of pride and end with a chapter on personal application. (Not how to apply pride to your life, but how to overcome it. Living at poverty level is one way, but not recommended). It's a basic explanation. The Seven Deadly Sins earned their notoriety because they are parents. As Pride begat Lust, Lust begat Adultery, Adultery begat Anger, Anger begat Murder, Murder begat 25 to life, etc. Or if you're single: Gluttony begat Alcoholism, Alcoholism begat Drunkenness, Drunkenness begat Fornication, Fornication begat My Baby's Daddy and on and on.

Oh, yeah, it's full of gems like that.

Finally, we send the acquisitions editor at the publishing house the sample chapters on pride. He really likes the tone, gives me a few suggestions and I go back and rewrite for another couple weeks. This is all on spec, by the way. Spec means you don't get paid unless they decide to make a deal. I'm not sure what spec is short for. Speculation? That's probably it. You're gambling on your talent. Well, honestly, in much of publishing you're only gambling on the strength of the idea. The Christian market, at least, doesn't publish for the sake of craft, but that's another issue. Anyway, my lit agent sends in the updated material and the acquisitions editor loves it. Says I've hit all the right notes. This is a winner. But there's no deal yet. Now, he has to take it to another team of acquisitions editors who will read it and decide if I get to advance to the next level. It's like a reality show that no one watches except my lit agent and me.

A week later, he calls my lit agent back to let us know that everyone on the team loves it. He says even some of the naysayers who thought I couldn't pull it off are impressed. That's hoop number one. This is going great. My lit agent and I consider high fiving each other. Thankfully, I live in California and he lives in New York, so we're spared this embarrassing cultural practice. We know we've got nothing yet, but this could be everything. I try not to think about the weight of debt being lifted off our shoulders if this pans out.

In the back of my mind, I suppress the temptation of certain fantasies, like adding up the advance per book of a seven book deal, carrying the zeroes and applying them to our newly developed budget, checking off the bills that we could wave goodbye to if this deal comes through. Sure, the thoughts pop in my mind, but I shake my head to erase them with the Etch A Sketch® brain with which God has blessed me. Still, there are flashes, glimpses in my mind, like my wife and I burning our Target Visa. Our little girls laughing in the background. We're standing on the porch of our beloved Victorian house, which we get to keep, by the way, because I've landed this seven-book deal.

I twist my neck from side to side to rid my mind of such thoughts. Refocus.

The next hoop is the marketing team. The acquisitions editor takes it to them to see if they think seven books is even a good idea. It's takes him a couple of weeks to meet with the head of marketing. The head of marketing says she'll have to read over what I've written.

Tune in next week.

Another week goes by.

The acquisitions guy calls my lit agent and says, "Marketing approved the series. They think seven books on the seven deadly sins will make a bigger splash than one book on the seven deadly sins."

We think so too.

Hoop number two is cleared.

The final hoop, he has to take the idea to the board for final approval. The word "board" has us all scared. They don't sound whimsical. They sound "board." We soon learn that the board will not be reading the sample chapters. The acquisitions editor will type a one-page synopsis of everything regarding this book idea and that's what the board will make their decision based upon. That's like hiring a comedian based upon someone else who has seen his show. In that scenario, the persona or the tone or the point of view is irrelevant. It's not lowbrow culture. It's no-brow culture, because it's only about the marketing. The question isn't, "Is this a unique voice that speaks into culture for the sake of the gospel?" The question is simply, "Will it sell?" This meeting is three weeks away. This is going to be a substantial investment, the acquisitions editor warns, but he's optimistic.

All we have to do now is wait.

Some more.

It's the season finale for our reality show.

In the meantime, I push away all thoughts that lend themselves to fantasizing about making a living as an author or any thoughts about how the advance on a seven book deal would pull us completely out of debt. *One day at a time, Sweet Jesus.*

My literary agent calls. It's the climax of the season finale.

"Good morning," he says flatly.

I ask him to hold a second so I can put my earbuds in, but I can tell from the way he said good morning that I should expect bad news.

"What's up?"

"The board said there's nothing funny about the seven deadly sins," he says.

Sure, give it to me straight.

Our instincts were right. They're not whimsical.

"Well, that's because they didn't read my sample chapters," I say.

"They rejected the idea outright."

I've been voted off the island. I don't get a rose. My phone-a-friend doesn't know the answer. Donald fires me. I'm the biggest loser. Or is the biggest loser the winner? Whatever. There's no deal.

Best face forward, I take the news with mild disappointment. I've heard the same line of reasoning before. *Comedy is frivolous.* It's hard to convince people otherwise. No one takes comedians seriously.

The word frivolous means "not having any serious purpose" and therein lies the misunderstanding. Some comedy is very serious. My first book satirized the thinking of the emerging church movement. It wasn't frivolous. Even God mocked nations. Psalm 59:8 reads, "But you, O LORD, laugh at them; you scoff at all those nations." Scoffing means mocking, ridiculing, making fun of, laughing at, poking fun at, trash talking, cracking, ranking on, woofin' and west coast dissin'. Still, we must remember it's never a good idea to say "yo' momma" to Jesus. The Catholics make a good point.

Anyway, I endure the shock and go about my day.

Until my evening prayer-walk.

It is my habit to take a walk around our neighborhood in the evening and pray during my walk. If it's still light out I slip my i-Phone's earbuds in so people don't think I'm nuts, walking around and talking to myself. During my evening walk it hits me. I am devastated. I feel a deep sense of loss. This confuses me, because I didn't spend anytime fantasizing about what would happen if they said yes to the deal. When the thoughts came, I pushed them away. Then I realized why it reached so deep. I had spent so much time researching and writing that this book idea became a big part of my life. Now it was gone.

This led to thoughts of my wife's miscarriages.

Before we had our first child, my wife miscarried twice. It was hard on me but even more devastating to her because she carried the children. I know losing a book deal is not the same as losing a child but that's what it felt like. I was pregnant with Septuplets. "You're going to have seven books."

And then the doctor walks in and tells me they're all dead.

Miscarriage.

I tried not to get my hopes up but it's difficult to detach yourself when you invest so much time and energy. All you're left with is the Land of Misfit Punchlines who have no place to call home.

Just a week before, I gave the Sunday sermon at our church and said, "If you're a Christian, really, what's the worst case scenario for your life? That you lose your home or reputation? That your spouse leaves you? That you're diagnosed with cancer? That someone kills you? If to live is Christ, there is no worst case scenario for a Christian."

We are going through the Apostle Paul's letter to the Philippians.

I understand the words.

I believe the words.

I just can't shake this depression.

For two days I am completely despondent, unable to pray without weeping over this loss of creative life. I go to my office to work and end up piddling around until noon when I realize that I'm not getting anything done. Snap out of it. That's what I tell myself anyway.

I take walks and talk to the Lord about it.

"Why are you so cast down, O my soul, and why are you in turmoil within me?" Giving myself pep talks, "Ah, you're in debt and you just lost a book deal that could have got you out. Shake it off. It's only a book deal. God continues to provide for the mortgage each month. You have a lovely, supportive wife who believes in you. Two children whose smiles ignite joy in you. It's only a book deal. A really, really, *really* good book deal. The heart of every person is in the hands of God. He could have swayed the board in another direction, in a whimsical direction. He did not and that is best."

I know this in my mind, but I am still dejected.

I pray for Jesus to pull me out of this.

He does.

Halfway through our slow trudge out of debt it feels much the same. There are setbacks and tiny bits of progress followed by more setbacks and, even after just under a year, sometimes it feels like we just can't make it. Especially after I receive a call that says the radio station is canceling the event in Nashville. We are counting on that money. Well, we were. It's not there anymore. My wife mentions thoughts of bankruptcy again. I say, "No." Then she says, "I know. God always shows me different." Then I receive a call and book another gig for the month. It looks like we'll make the mortgage after all.

I don't feel dejected anymore.

Sure, I still feel this cloud of debt over my head, but at least I can look up.

I know where my help comes from.

12

THE NEW AMERICAN DREAM
(Loan Modification)

◆◆◆◆◆◆◆◆◆◆◆◆◆◆

The web site for the California Housing Finance Agency features a slogan: "Keep Your Home." That's a good slogan.

So far, so good.

Below the slogan is a photo of a couple standing outside of their home with their arms around each other, their backs to us, looking at their home.

It makes me wonder.

Did they get to keep their home?

I can't see their faces. I don't know if they're happy or shooting tears like a squirt gun. If that picture is meant to convey a happy ending, well, it fails. It's ambivalent. They're outside. Are they taking one last look at their home?

If the folks at CHFA want to create a feeling of security in potential home losers, they should show a photo of a couple sleeping in bed with smiles on their faces. I can only imagine so many scenarios for that and they're all good.

I checked out the web site because my mortgage company (GMAC) just told me to call back in 15 minutes. I guess they're a little busy these days. To kill time, they told me to check out the web site www.

makinghomesaffordable.com, which is where I see the backs of this couple who may or may not get to keep their home.

After mulling over the site, I call back and listen to the options the robot secretary gives me and then listen to Kenny G music for about five minutes. To avoid dealing with us, maybe their goal is to drive us to suicide. Hence, Kenny G music.

Someone finally answers.

When I tell her I want to talk to someone about a loan modification, she tells me to call the number I just called to reach her. I'm not making this up. "That's the number I just called," I say.

"Let me connect you."

"Okay."

She connects me to the number I just called... again.

Robot lady: *Call back later, our system is still down.*

According to the reliability of their system and the familiarity of the employees with their whereabouts, I'm not getting my hopes up.

I give it 30 minutes before I call back.

System's still down. Guess their IT guy didn't show up today.

They ask for 30 minutes this time. I graciously give them an extension, hoping they'll get the hint.

My wife and I are now in the position to refinance our home. It's been three years. While waiting in line at Starbucks, I'm told by a random stranger that it's extremely difficult to refinance your home. (Here I thought I was praying quietly under my breath, "Help us refinance our home, Lord." But I guess the guy in front of me heard me.) It can be difficult to refinance your home? Not at all what our trusty Christian real estate agent told us. She's no brother-in-law. Then someone else in line tells me that agents received kickbacks by promoting these ARM loans. "Will you people please stop eavesdropping on my prayers!"

Refinancing is not something I'm looking forward to because every story I've heard (in line at Starbucks anyway) has included a minimum of 250 phone calls to the mortgage company dealing with different people each call. I wonder if they'll ask me about how much

I spend on Starbucks. I thank my barista for the financial lesson and head back home.

Later, I call back.

Ring, ring.

Robot lady.

Press number two.

Kenny G.

Suicidal thoughts.

Then a real lady answers and asks, "Are you calling about (unintelligible) program for refinancing?"

"I don't know," I say. "I'm calling about whatever programs are available for refinancing."

She informs me in a very slight but unidentifiable accent that the Obama administration has a program to prevent homeowners from becoming home losers. She doesn't use those words, but that's the idea. If this turns out to be true and works, President Obama will be my all-time favorite President. I don't care what my mother-in-law says.

"Can you answer a series of questions about your financial status?" she asks.

"Yes."

"Can you make this month's payment?"

Darn it.

We just made this month's payment, thanks to God's miracle of two last minute gigs during the same weekend.

"Yes," I say dejectedly, expecting to be disqualified immediately.

"Would you like me to set up payment now?"

"Ah, we just paid it. Today. This morning."

"Okay," she says trusting my check's in the mail speech, which just so happens to be true.

"Have you experienced a change in income?" she asks

"Yes. I'm self-employed and with the change in the economy and the implosion of my booking agency I'm not making as much this year."

"That's okay, Sir. Don't worry. I'm here to help you."

"Thank you. I am here to be helped."

"One of the requirements you will need to fulfill to qualify for a loan modification is a hardship letter. Can you write a letter?"

"Dear Phone Support Lady, yes I can. Sincerely, Thor Ramsey."

She doesn't laugh, so I'll assume she just smiles. It's the comedian's way.

"Do you occupy the property?"

"Yes. Mostly I occupy the couch, but that is on the property."

Then she asks me about our monthly income and if we happen to have $25,000 or more in gold bricks, bonds, savings or other such things.

"I just lost a seven book deal," I tell her.

"That's okay, Sir. I'm here to help you."

I get the feeling she's reading off a script.

Then she says in a very strong New York Bronx accent, "You don't understand! I coulda had class. I coulda been a contender. I could've been somebody, instead of a bum, which is what I am."

Yeah, she's definitely reading off a script.

She tells me to go to their web site and fill out a financial analysis form. I want to ask her if that couple on the web site gets to keep their home. We have 15 days to complete the form. "Send it in as quickly as possible because it takes us 30 days to respond. Do you have any questions?"

"No," I say, feeling hopeful, assuming everything worked out for that web couple.

Keep your home.

That's a good slogan.

Two weeks later we receive a short letter saying that they've received our paperwork and will respond in 20 days. That's good news, because the deadline for this book is around 20 days away, which means I'll be able to finish this chapter. I pray for a happy ending. But however it goes, it will be a happy ending, right? If all things work together for the good of those who love God and are called according to his purposes, then it's all good. It's amazing how cheery you can be once you embrace God's sovereignty. (In hindsight, I now realize God was using these trials to prepare us for even greater trials. I did not realize I was going to be pastoring and preaching soon and very soon.)

I'll be back in 20 days with the news.

Or sooner.

⌘

I'm back.

We heard back in about a week.

They said they didn't receive all the documents needed, specifically our business profit & loss statements for the last three months. The disheartening thing is that I sent them six months of our profit & loss statements with all the other paperwork we filled out for them. I don't know why this surprises me because the first person I spoke with didn't even know her own location.

So, I re-fax the statements and tomorrow I'll follow-up with a phone call to make sure they received everything. If they don't receive all the paperwork, they just assume you're good to go. "Never mind about that loan modification, guys. I don't know what I was thinking."

I call them back the next day and another robot secretary says, "Thank you for calling. Your call will be answered in less than one-minute. Commercial, blah, blah, blah. Please ask your account representative if you may benefit."

Then a human lady answers.

I never get names. If they give names I don't hear them. It's just something I lose between the transition from robot to human. Anyway, the human tells me they did receive our profit & loss statements. Then she laughs and says, "More like loss statements, Bud." I think. That's what I hear in my head anyway. It's probably not on tape even though our conversation was recorded for quality control.

"Can I help you with anything else?"

"Well, I have to ask… do I benefit?"

"I'm sorry?"

"The robot said to ask if I benefit."

"The robot?"

"The human voice without a person attached."

"I'm sorry, Sir. I'm not sure I understand."

"That's okay," I say, happy to be misunderstood by a human being. "This conversation won't go in my file, will it?"

"No."

"Thank you then. Hope to hear some good news from you in 20 days."

"I hope so, too."

"Goodbye, Human Lady."

∽

Later that same year…

GMAC sends us two letters informing us that… we'll, honestly, I'm not sure what they're informing us because the letters were written by lawyers. I think the first letter says that our loan modification has been denied because we're rich enough. Only a lawyer knows for sure.

Then we receive another letter dated two weeks later that says they modified our loan on a trial bases. I think. It appears we only have to pay half our mortgage payment for three months and then our "situation will be reviewed to determine the best option," such as a short sale.

A short sale?

This is California, so people do dress casually. Who knows? Maybe selling shorts can keep us in our home. Our mortgage company seems to think so. Maybe Obama's plan to save homes is a yard sale of summer clothes.

To clarify things, I call GMAC and even the guy I talk to isn't sure about the letters. He isn't a lawyer, either. He suggests I just make the partial payments. My wife just sent in a full payment and they applied it to two months. He says this in itself may disqualify us.

"Call back Friday to see if you've been disqualified," he suggests.

So, the message they seem to be sending is – you're better off if you just stop making your payments, because that'll give you a better shot at a loan modification.

I don't want to wait until Friday, so I call back and speak to someone else for further clarification. She says that we're setup for a loan modification on a trial basis. Okay, but what does that mean? A trial basis? Do we get back to them? "Hey, we tried out that paying less per month thing. I think we like it." Is that it?

Or is it from their perspective. "Hey, we tried out that receiving less money each month thing. We don't like it."

Well, right now, we'll know in three months if our trial works out. I'd ask you to pray for us, but by the time this is in print we'll either be modified or you can look forward to my next book – *The Short Sale (or Bake Sales & Other Ideas to Make Your Mortgage Payment)*.

Regardless, we have to figure out some way to make our mortgage payment. This is where the morality of the housing bust comes into play. If you do a casual search on Google for "housing bust" you will find one analyst who insists that homeowners have no more obligation to make their payments than banks that walk away from bad investments without moral wobbling and the next analyst says that each family needs to evaluate their options with abandonment as last on the list and on and on with differing opinions and advice. The housing bust is something God has used like a big highlighter across our country – *here's the problem, little children.* As a country, we've lost our moral common sense.

This shouldn't be news to most Christians, but thanks to the errors of the prosperity, name it and claim it, health and wealth gospel, I'm afraid it is.

So, the big question becomes, "Why should we feel morally obligated to sacrifice to make payments to a bank that feels no obligation toward us?" For the Christian, the answer is plain and simple, if not unnerving: Because however we treat someone else is how we treat God.

Are banks our neighbor?

Should we love our enemies?

The answers are Vacation Bible School 101, which isn't a bad idea. Maybe everyone involved in the housing bust needs to go back to Vacation Bible School because a little moral common sense goes a long way.

Unlike an adjustable rate mortgage.

THE BROKE DENTAL PLAN
(Chew On the Side That Doesn't Hurt)
••••••••••••••

When it comes to saving money, the only thing my wife and I have going for us is a life insurance policy that my mother set up that names me as the beneficiary. When she dies, I get some money. *And she gets the cheapest funeral possible.* Don't worry. My mother and I have discussed this and it's really what she wants. She doesn't believe in wasting money on something you'll only use once, like a casket.

My wife had a 401K through the company she worked for but that has since liquidated. So, thanks to my mother, that life insurance policy is it, which is not a strategy most financial counselors encourage – waiting for someone to die. Using life insurance policies as a means of savings can make you root for someone's death and if they get wind of this while they're alive they can still change the name of the beneficiary. *(Don't worry, Sis, your secret's safe with me.)*

Saving money is something my wife and I have never agreed on. We have no financial plan. Shoot. We have no dental plan. I am a self-employed standup comedian. Our dental plan is – chew on the side that doesn't hurt. It's a two part plan: plan A, the right cheek, plan B, the left cheek. Choose one.

In our early marriage we maintained separate checking accounts, splitting all the costs as if we were roommates. At the time, my wife had a higher paying job than I did, so I suggested we save my income and live off hers. She didn't like the idea and I didn't humbly lead. I just mildly suggested it as a co-dependent. Part of the reason I was quiet was the separateness of our accounts. And part of the reason was that *she made way more than I did*. We were not yet living as one flesh. We weren't even living as one checkbook. Living as one flesh doesn't mean you have to use each other's toothbrush, something my wife cannot stomach to this day. It just means that if you're not of one mind on this topic, then you're not going to be saving any money.

The other part of our problem was that I was not leading our home spiritually. Well, I thought I was, but have come to realize years later that I was not. Had I actually been leading our home I would have led my wife down to the bank and opened a savings account.

One way to save money is by having a simple rule of paying yourself first. It's a basic plan taught by many financial gurus. When you get paid, you put 10 percent in savings, you give 10 percent to church and you use the rest to live on. You pay yourself first by putting money into savings. Be careful though, because I've fallen behind in paying myself and now I'm in debt with myself for $100,000. Unfortunately, I've turned myself over to a collection agency but they can't seem to get ahold of me.

Just make sure you get the order right.

The thing about nearing the end of your goals is that even this close to the end you'll find small setbacks, like you'll get word that your mother is still alive. Then there's the bad news you receive when you're out of town. In a hotel room somewhere, I hear my phone chime in the middle of the night that I have a text. Groggily, I peek through the darkness of unfamiliar surroundings and find my cell. The text is from my wife: "Pray. Heart beat is not right."

My wife was born with a heart murmur and during the birth of our first child the OBGYN said, "It was the first time in my career that I feared for the life of the mother." He thought he was going to lose her. He even told her to tell me goodbye, but she decided against it, like you can tell death, "No thank you." She said, "God didn't bring me this far to let me die." That's good to hear, since she's afraid of dying tonight. Since the birth of our first child she has been on heart medication.

Naturally, her text concerns me. I pray and text her back: "Praying for you now." Then she texts back: "I'm scared." So, I text: "I'm calling you," because I don't want the ring to scare her to death. That would be bad.

She doesn't sound so good on the phone.

"Go to the emergency room," I say.

"I can't. We don't have health insurance."

"What?"

"Honey," she explains, "We haven't had health insurance for the last year. It was $700 a month."

I guess we haven't been talking about financial matters as much as we should. Now that things are looking up financially for us, we have to get this health care business squared away. Otherwise we won't be leaving our children an inheritance because my wife has no life insurance policy, either. If I die, they're covered. If she dies... I can't even afford to bury her right now. I'd have to leave her in one of the cars I abandoned in a parking lot somewhere. At least we'd have a place to leave flowers. We've never even discussed the possibility of her dying. I don't even know what her wishes would be if she died. I can't imagine she wants to be buried out back by the cat. But that would be our only other option at this point.

I don't know much about insurance, but this is the first time in my life I've even considered sitting down with an insurance salesman, pushing the play *Death of a Salesman* out of my thoughts because that's my image of insurance salesmen – like an evening with Death.

You see why getting out of debt and staying out of debt is so vital? My wife has been neglecting her health to avoid a $700 a month health insurance payment because we weren't money enough ahead to pay it. Being in debt could cost you your life.

I pray for her over the phone and she says she's going to try to get some sleep. "I'm leaving at four-thirty this morning," I say, "so let me know how you are if you're up."

Then I try to sleep.

I get another text at 4:21: "Okay right now to sleep." I text back: "Keep me updated. I don't wanna lose you." *Who will find all the stuff I misplace?*

My ride drops me off at the Oakland airport. Just after checking in, I get a text from my wife: "I'm hoping Daniel can listen to it today and tell me something. It is beating so weird." Daniel is a member of our church who is doing his residency as a budding young doctor. He has a stethoscope in his car, which comes in handy whenever my wife is about to die.

I text her: "Have you not been asleep yet?"

"I slept an hour. When I picked Kate up from crying it got worse."

"Call me."

She sounds worse and can't talk for long.

It's Sunday, the day we normally struggle with tithing, not health issues. It seems things like this always come into play when we consider how much to tithe. "Well, we have this new doctor bill and that expense and whatnot and so forth." It always becomes an issue: "How much do we give away, especially when times are tough?"

Sometimes our intention is to tithe, but we delay one-week and it gets eaten up by other things, especially if you're living from paycheck to paycheck and discover your wife might have to go to the hospital. Suddenly, our tithe is being reallocated to pay for a trip to urgent care, which she texts me "opens at 7 a.m."

I text her: "Go. I'm boarding. Talk to you when I land. Love you!"

When it comes to tithing, it's always something.

This is why so many of us are surprised when we get to the end of the year and discover how little we've given to the church. We had no idea we fell in that 5 percent and under category. We felt like we were being generous. Many times we want to give, but we are so poorly organized that it becomes, "Hey, did we tithe on this check already?"

"I dunno. I think so."

Yeah, we better not give *again*. That might be *too* much.

One moment I'm encouraged by our financial situation, the next moment I'm worried. This health insurance issue is exactly the kind of thing that can keep us from giving. "How much was your doctor bill?" I don't know yet and that's where the temptation to hold back comes in. Maybe you're maxed out on debt and feel like you have nothing to give, that it would be irresponsible to give at this point. Oh, *now* we want to get responsible with our money – when there's giving involved.

Situations like this are not uncommon. We neglected to tithe before for one reason or another. And every reason feels like this present one, like a crisis. After we missed tithing one week, the next week I received a call from someone who was producing a show at the Comedy Store in Hollywood. When they called me for the gig, they stressed it was a fundraiser for a worthy cause like a water supply for kids somewhere. After I told them what my standard honorarium was, I said, "But I'll leave it up to you what you decide to pay me, since it's just in L.A." Now, I wasn't expecting anywhere near my standard honorarium, but my thinking was that I would take this check (which I assumed would be about 10 percent of what I normally get) and use it for our Sunday tithe. You know? A makeup tithe. After the show, I opened the little thank you envelope they gave me to behold a $5 Starbucks' gift card. That was the first time I've ever been disappointed by Starbucks in my life.

It was disappointing and depressing to not give that Sunday.

Always send a contract, no matter what. It clarifies things, like you expect to be paid in American dollars rather than coffee beans.

Later, she still doesn't feel well so she goes to urgent care. There is no cardiologist available, so the guy at urgent care wants to call an ambulance and send her to the hospital. You know, so they don't get sued. My wife asks the guy what he is basing all this on and his only answer is the heart murmur she's had since childhood. "That's it?" she says to him. "No, I can't go with that. I'll go see my own cardiologist tomorrow. I'm not paying to have an ambulance take me to the hospital where we'll have to pay for staying, not to mention all the tests." And with that, she hands him the complimentary paper dress and leaves.

"How do you feel now?" I ask.

"I chewed up an aspirin. My heart feels normal now."

This is one gutsy lady.

I am both thankful and appalled. Thankful that she didn't go to the hospital for the night and appalled that she didn't go to the hospital for the night. But that's our situation. She said to the urgent care guy, "This could break our family financially." So, she took an aspirin. They're cheaper. It falls right in line with our "chew on the side that doesn't hurt" dental policy.

Insurance is a lot more important than most of us care to admit. I never imagined that whether or not we had health insurance would ever play a part in our tithing. When my wife and I decided to get out of debt we both determined that we would give the standard 10 percent tithe of every check. Sometimes before I write that tithe check I experience an inner spiritual battle. On days like today, that's when I have to remind myself of certain biblical truths, such as "he who did not spare his own Son but gave him up for us all, how will he not also with him graciously give us all things?"[10] I remind myself that the promise is for "all things" including my family's wellbeing, that I can give freely and not withhold. God will take care of us and our necessities, our daily bread. If we need heat, he'll provide heat. If we need health insurance, he'll provide for it. If we need a grande light mocha frappuccino, well, we're on our own.

So, I write the check and pray, thanking God that he is good to us and will take care of us. I don't usually write it during the church service because I don't carry a checkbook around with me.

I'm no dummy.

I write it at home where I can always change my mind.

---

10 Romans 8:32

14

SLACKER BE THY NAME
(The Recline of the Protestant Work Ethic)
♦♦♦♦♦♦♦♦♦♦♦♦♦♦

Now I hope you realize that the thing that will build enough wealth for you to be generous is your income. In other words, work builds wealth. Not fancy investment tricks. Just plain old hard work. That's right. Work is the preferred method of building wealth as lottery tickets have proven unreliable and full of false hope. You buy a handful and start scraping away. "My life's gonna be great – SCRAPE, SCRAPE – if poor equals great."

"We're gonna take a cruise – SCRAPE, SCRAPE – around the block, in the car."

"I'm gonna throw a big party – SCRAPE, SCRAPE – for all my invisible friends."

Things like the lottery are subtle because you don't lose all your money at once. Now that would make the lottery exciting if there was some actual risk involved when you played. You scratch away and it says, "You owe $10,000." Now *that* would be losing the lottery. Besides, most lottery winners live out Solomon's proverb: "Wealth gained hastily will dwindle, but whoever gathers little by little will increase it."[11]

---

11 Proverbs 13:11

There are two great tragedies in life: winning the lottery and not winning the lottery. Counting on something like the lottery is a lazy way to getting out of debt.

Work is the best method of building wealth. And it's greatest threat is laziness.

I've given this whole lazy thing some thought because my line of work lends itself to slacking off, as do most careers of the self-employed. If you're your own boss how much trouble can you get in if you just don't show up for work? I've thought about slackers long and hard while sitting at Starbucks, doodling on napkins. Consequently, I've doodled so many thoughts about slackers that it really amounts to a short bonus book inside the book you're reading now. How often do you get that? And you thought only DVDs came with extras.

Here are my observations about slackers everywhere via napkin doodles.

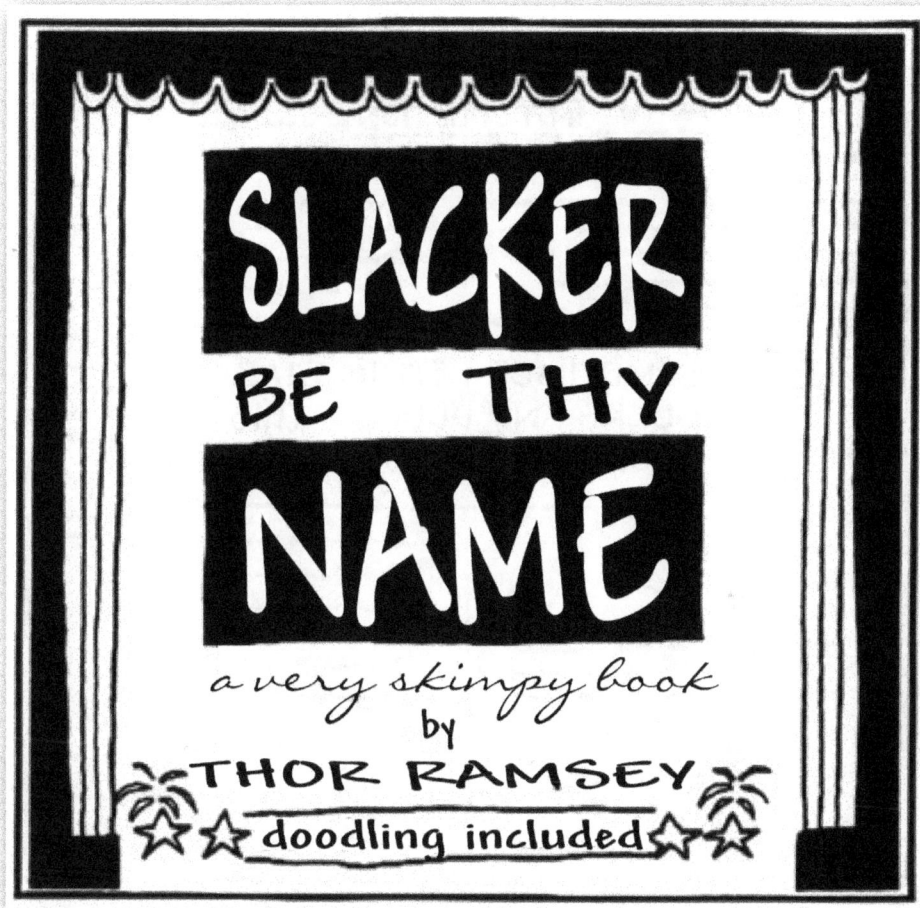

SLACKER BE THY NAME

a very skimpy book
by
THOR RAMSEY
☆☆ doodling included ☆☆

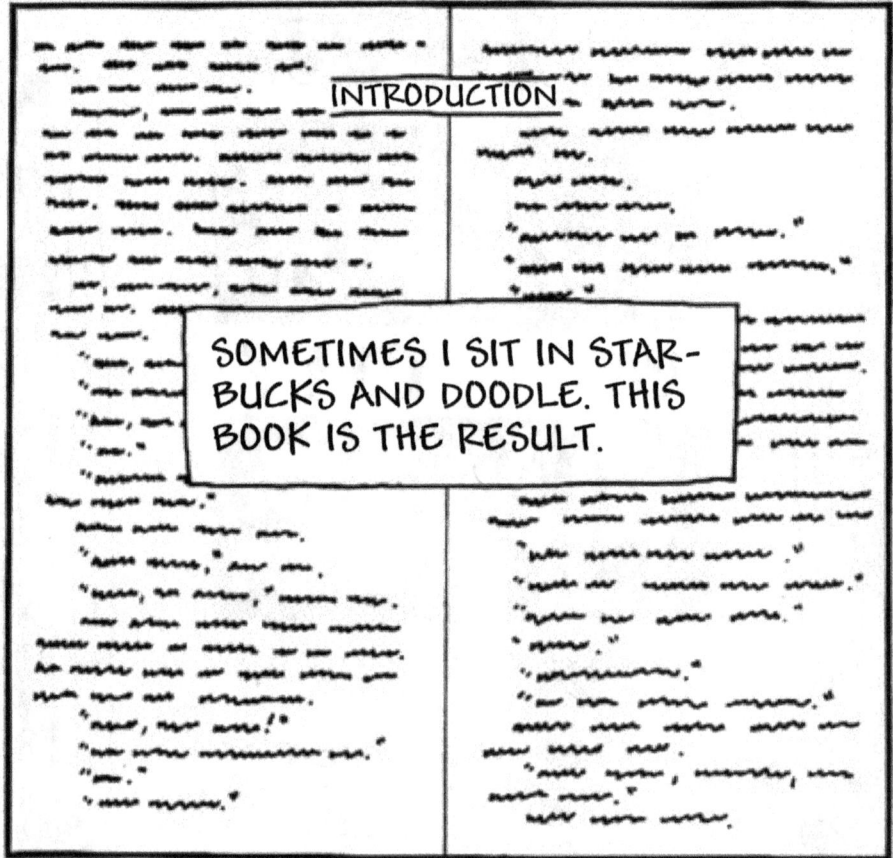

... PER

PAGE.

SLACKER \SLAK -ɜR\ N: A PERSON WHO SHIRKS WORK OR OBLIGATION. I.E. WHEN YOU DROP AN ICE-CUBE, IF YOU KICK IT UNDER THE FRIDGE —— SLACKER.

MAYBE YOU'D LIKE TO KNOW IF YOU'RE A SLACKER. HERE'S HOW YOU CAN TELL. IT'S A SIMILAR FORMULA TO THOSE OLD RED-NECK BOOKS. (THERE ARE NO NEW IDEAS WITH LAZY PEOPLE. THINKING IS HARD WORK.)

IF THE ONLY TIME YOU
CLEAN YOUR APARTMENT
IS WHEN YOU WANT YOUR
DEPOSIT BACK... SLACKER
BE THY NAME.

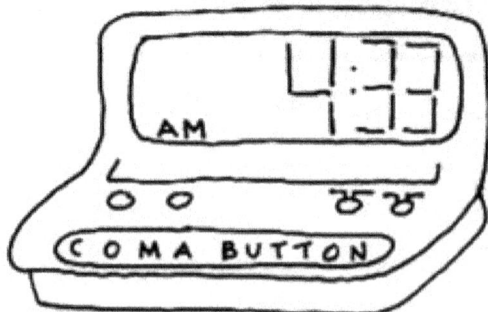

THANKS FOR READING MY PRETEND BOOK. IT WAS MUCH EASIER TO WRITE THAN A REAL BOOK, NOT TO DISPARAGE CARTOONISTS. I'M SURE DOODLING HAS ITS CHALLENGES, TOO.

If you find yourself defined by four or more of the above characterizations, then you are likely headed for a life of financial ruin or stand-up comedy. In many cases, both. So, find something to do. I suggest anything. And do it every day. That's diligence. That's the opposite of being a slacker. That's work. That's what most of our parents did so we wouldn't have to... which is a bad idea. Don't leave your children money. Leave them a business where they have to work for money. Leave your children land or your home or your business, but don't leave them so much that they become rich slackers. As it has been wisely said, the last check you write in your life should go to the undertaker and that one should bounce. *Sorry, kids.*

Being that we're Protestants, it would be wise to recover the Protestant work ethic to stop the tide of slackers slacking. Somehow our Protestant work ethic has been removed like a guy trying to smoke at a restaurant in California. I don't know what happened, but somehow there was a generation that neglected to pass it onto their children so the next generation missed it by default. Some blame it on the Baby Boomers whose parents indulged them. I am one of those children.

I've discovered that if you let your children complain their way out of things they become lazy. In our love, we are unintentionally breeding a generation of slackers who have no concept that being Protestant means having a work ethic.

This is why the Bible makes fun of slackers.

Just listen to some of these barbs.

Proverbs 6:6 - "Go to the ant, O sluggard; consider her ways, and be wise."

Kids aren't learning these lessons from ants today, because they don't play outside anymore.

Proverbs 19:24 - "The sluggard buries his hand in the dish and will not even bring it back to his mouth." If you're fasting because you're too lazy to feed yourself... How lazy can you be? So lazy that you'd starve if you had to put your hand to your mouth I guess. This is not far from the truth. (Probably why it's in the Bible.) It seems that a lazy person's goal in life is to avoid movement, specifically the movement of bending over. Be honest. Even now when you drop something do you give a grunt of annoyance because you have to bend over to pick it up? That's the type of slacking Solomon is writing about here. You drop an ice-cube, let out that grunt of annoyance and then... just kick it under the fridge.

Proverbs 22:13 - The sluggard says, "There is a lion outside! I shall be killed in the streets!" Slackers are always making excuses about why they can't do something. It's not that they can't get up and go to work. It's that there's a lion outside. Possibly. You never know. The city has a zoo. Be safe. Stay in bed.

God's will is that we work diligently and by pampering our children... well, I was going to write that we're losing our Protestant work ethic, but it's too late. It's lost. We have to regain it.

Let's start by stopping this talk of retirement.

What kind of message is that?

Retirement is not biblical. The Bible's idea of retirement is that we die. That's retirement. We don't work hard so we can stop working to wear yellow pants and saddle shoes with cleats. The mentality that we retire so we can play demonstrates just how lost our work ethic is. If we retire it should be *to* something else, not away from work. We retire so we can devote more time to ministry. We retire so we can start some new productive venture. But we don't just stop. That will not only kill us, but it's immoral. Retirement is the ultimate sin of omission.

Sorry, Gramps.

So, it's not only good to work, but it's God's will to work. That's why we do the best job that we can, because it's for him. Because whatever kind of job we do will reflect upon the One we follow, either positively or negatively. And he wants our work to reflect him because we will influence someone by doing it.

Proverbs 22:29 - "Do you see a man skillful in his work, he will stand before Kings. He will not stand before obscure men." The more excellent your work is (whatever it is) the more it will take you places you never thought possible. When I first started a career in standup comedy, an older wiser comedian took me aside and asked me this question, "How much time do you spend working on your act each day?"

"What?"

I didn't understand the question.

"This is comedy. It's not work," I thought.

Then he laid some enlightenment on me. He said, "Most comedians are so lazy they don't work on their acts at all. The comedians who do are the comedians who succeed. A really funny naturally talented but lazy comedian will eventually be passed up by a mildly funny guy who works really hard at it. He'll eventually become funnier than the more naturally talented guy, even if he only devotes two hours a day to his act."

Who knew?

Dying is easy. Comedy is hard.

That's true in whatever career you find yourself. Hard work pays off, not that two hours a day is hard work, but his example was relative. Two hours a day is hard work to lazy people.

So, find something to do.

Then do it like you're doing it for God Almighty (because you are). This means showing up on time, not stealing things from work, doing the best job you can no matter what that job is, etc.

Do it diligently. (This means showing up daily.)

And finally, do it honestly.

Proverbs 20:23 - "Unequal weights are an abomination." This is probably one of the most neglected areas of the Christian life. Most often, we think of this as having to do with "not stealing stuff from work and being fair." That's part of it. The other part has to do with the quality of our work. If we don't give a job our all then it's like stealing from our employer or our client or whoever we happen to work for. Giving a job just enough to get by. That's not honest. That's unequal weights.

And that's what happened to the Protestant work ethic – it lost its ethic. There's no morality to work anymore. People don't see the lack of effort they give their job as immoral. Welcome to the age of the Hedonistic Work Ethic where children only mow the lawn when it's fun. We lost our work ethic because we no longer view "whoever we work for" as Almighty God.

When we stand before God we want him to say, "Well done, good and faithful servant," not "slacker be thy name."

15

CAN I GET OUT OF DEBT?
(Before This Book is Published?)
••••••••••••••

For joy!

Last week we made a final click online, sending a $7,500 check to pay off a final credit card balance. It was a great feeling, even though there was no celebration music. I felt very encouraged about our financial situation. So much so that I spent 99 cents on a song from i-Tunes, played it for my wife and spun her around in front of the dryer.

Then I thought about last month, how much we took in, how many debts we paid off. It filled me with even more determination to stay out of debt because I also thought about how much we could have saved if not for all the debt. For example, we could have saved $7,500. That's something we paid in addition to necessities like Starbucks and the mortgage.

That's the thing about money.

Rich people have more of it.

This reality doesn't seem to change.

Since they have money, they talk about what to do with it, like mutual funds and Mid Cap funds and the S&P Index and Emerging Markets and other things that people like me, with no money, have no idea what they're talking about when they refer to their hedgehog.

Is a mutual fund a fund my wife and I have in common? I assume. Mid Cap, some sort of investment in ball caps, not a large investment, not a small investment, but a mid-investment. It's just right. S&P Index could be anything. Shooting & Pistols Index. Socks & Pajamas Index. Sorry & Pardon's Index, the index used to measure scandals of political figures.

During our climb out of debt, some days I felt hopeful about the future and some days I faced our bills: TWENTY different creditors, including hospital, dental and credit card bills. Not to mention the $4.69 that I owed my mother-in-law for eating her bag of Doritos. And it can happen again just like that. Emergency health issue and boom – you're in debt. (Well, at least now I know the difference between a caffeine buzz and high blood pressure.)

The fact that we're out of debt is absolutely amazing if you noticed how dumb we were about money matters. (See the book you're reading now, mostly any page.) Amazing grace that saved a dunce like me. While I was writing this book, my editor kept asking me, "Do you think you'll be out of debt by the time the book is published?"

And I would always answer with an unequivocal, "No."

Sure, I understood that it would make a tidy ending to a book about getting out of debt if the author got out of debt, but I couldn't promise that. The book was more about exposing our guts and not giving up while encouraging others to do the same. Letting people know there will be peaks and valleys and that someone else was going through the same thing. All because we were taken in by a false gospel, shaped by the liturgical practices of the local mall.

Because finances can be so depressing, I didn't look at our bank account regularly. I knew our budget plan: spend less, pay down the debt. So, when I discovered that we owed half as much as I thought we did I was ecstatic because that's the same day I discovered we could eliminate our debt.

For joy.

I remember the day my wife and I discovered we had enough cash to pay down our major credit cards. She told me what she wanted to do with the money, then I told her what I wanted to do with the money and we experienced something new – a fight about *having* money. Suddenly, bank statements are fun to read. We could eliminate all of our major credit cards. Hint: *all* our credit cards are major credit cards. It's not like we have a *Dippin' Dots* credit card. It's the ice-cream of the future. So, they'll scan the mark on your forehead. Watch out for that.

But it's true. We were able to reduce our debt significantly by *paying everything off*. One simple step that only took a year. *It's a really long step.* Then we burned the invoices while my wife and children prepared the s'mores. "Are you cold, children? Let me burn some more credit cards applications."

We made it out of the hole in just over a year. Don't you love a good underdog story? Aren't you a Chargers fan? (They're a football team.) I'm told Harry Potter is an underdog, but no one who has magical powers is an underdog. That's not even fair. But we all love underdog stories because most of us have been underdogs at some point in our lives. We can relate to the saga of the underdog: someone in unfavorable conditions struggling to overcome great odds. Sometimes we just have to overcome being odd first, which makes us even more of an underdog.

As an underdog in debt, that's what it's going to feel like. It's going to feel like a good disaster movie. It's like your luxury liner hit this huge glacier called debt and your world is sinking. You have to abandon ship. Now, you're bouncing around the ocean, feeling cold and alone, waiting for the sharks to eat you (or loan officers). But you slowly begin the long swim to shore. That's the paying down of debt. It feels like you're not making progress, but you keep paddling your feet anyway. Then 18 months later, you reach dry land. It's not easy, but once you reach dry land, you jump around and run to your spouse in slow motion on the beach. You probably wouldn't have been in this situation to begin with if you hadn't had a luxury liner. Who can afford boats these days? Sell the boat. Pay down your debt. Run toward her in slow motion someplace less expensive next time.

Maybe you're beginning this journey as an underdog, too. Good for you. Become your own underdog story. As an underdog, doggedly pursue a debt-free life. The important thing is you have taken a step toward financial recovery by reading this book. (Or at least I have now that you bought my book. Thanks for that.) Don't worry, Underdog, you can do it. You can get out of debt and begin to build wealth and in fifteen years you can be a millionaire. If you happen to be alive in fifteen years, then no problem. But don't let death get you down… assuming you're a Christian.

People will tell you it can't be done, but ignore my mother-in-law. If by reading this book you continue to follow your plan of getting out of debt, then this is by far the best humor book you've ever read. I'd recommend it to many friends and relatives if I were you, especially if they're the same people who've been telling you for years that it's impossible to live debt-free. I'm telling you it can be done. I've discovered that it takes many people telling you the same things repeatedly before you begin to believe them. Things like, "Take my advice and dump him." Things like that. (Thankfully, my wife never took their advice.) That's just the first sign of hope. After you believe them, you take action. Sometimes. Maybe you think about taking action for a few years and then a recession hits, your booking agency implodes, your wife's 401K vanishes and then you find yourself without any money.

Boy, does your life stink.

Wait.

That's my life.

In any case, the point is the end of this book could be the beginning of another for you. I hope this book has either encouraged you in your journey to financial recovery or inspired you to begin. You will experience highs and lows as you pay off your bills, get out of debt and begin to forge a new financial future as a new champion of capital instead of an underdog of debt. Or a king of cash instead of a chump of change. Or a gold medalist of gold instead of a dark horse of dinero. Or a… you get the idea, I own a thesaurus. (Just one of the advantages of having money.)

It takes commitment, but if you keep at it you'll begin to notice changes not only with your checkbook, but with you. Like your nails get longer when you have money. Your spouse appears more attractive when they're not yelling at you about the disconnected phone. Things like that.

Before we were broke, I had enough frequent flyer miles for two first-class roundtrip tickets to New York City where I had planned to take my wife for a getaway weekend to take in a Broadway show, do some shopping and fly home. Then our priorities changed. We never did take that trip. I eventually used those miles for work to save travel expenses to help pay down our debt. Sure, I'd like to do that trip someday, but I told myself, "Now is not the time. There's nothing good playing on Broadway."

And I can honestly say this, if I had to do it all over again – I would've taken my wife to New York. I don't look back on those flights now with any fond memory. I can't even remember what gigs they were for now. Get out of debt, but don't be stupid about it. The financial gurus, who are very helpful in terms of what steps to take, can make you feel incredibly guilty for enjoying a weekend getaway with your spouse. Don't let them do that to you. That's a horrible way to live. Yet, we were committed to a lifestyle of getting out of debt and that's why we never went to New York. In hindsight, it does make a difference. Who knows? Had we taken that trip to New York maybe we would have compromised on other financial matters and found ourselves discouraged again. It's just that memories of sacrifice are not always fond memories. The crucifixion is a wonderful thing for those of us who have come to know Christ, but I'd be reticent to say that Jesus looks back upon his crucifixion as a fond memory. He endured it for the joy set before him, which was doing the Father's will. The joy set before us was getting out of debt, which isn't quite as motivating as saving people's souls.

The point is, you have to make some tough choices.

While checking out my rental car this last weekend, the rental guy asks me if I'd like to upgrade to the next level of car for just five dollars a day. Before I started on this journey to a debt-free existence I would have gone for the extra room. My family is meeting me in Grand Rapids this week and we'll be on the road two-weeks. That's the reason I wanted to give myself for upgrading. *We need more space.* The real reason was that I didn't want to be seen driving a PT Cruiser. Have you seen this confused vehicle? It looks like it was in a time travel accident. But I gratefully decline, keeping the PT Cruiser, which apparently only rental car agencies buy. (My apologies if you happen to own one. I'm sure you've learned from your mistake.) What does the PT stand for? Personal Tragedy... for buying it? Physical Training... from pushing it? Maybe it means Part Time car.

Then I'm at the Apple Store having my iPhone serviced by a genius when I notice a nice new Hurley laptop backpack. My backpack is frayed and split at the bottom, but it still holds the laptop. So far. The new backpack is eighty bucks and I just deposited seven checks from the last two-weeks into the bank. I can afford it. I can pay cash. But I don't.

When we arrive home, my wife hands our pastor's wife a check and says, "I'm giving this cheerfully. In case you can't tell. I'm very cheerful."

These are all good signs of heart transformation. Well, besides my wife gritting her teeth. Like all true spiritual growth, the radical shifts take time.

I am more like you than any financial guru you've ever read. I've gone from underdog to underdog out of debt. That should fill you with hope for the future. It hasn't been easy living out these practical little principles, but it has been worth it.

Aside from missing that trip to New York.

Keep at it, my friend.

For joy.

ACKNOWLEDGEMENTS

This book would have been impossible without my wife, of course, who could have killed the whole project simply by refusing to use cash. As always, but probably not mentioned enough, aloud, in front of dinner guests, I am grateful for her support in all creative endeavors.

For the third time in a row, the skillful mechanics of Marshall Allen's insightful editorial eye fixed this thing up good. Keen in his double role as literary agent, he gives me such scrupulous attention that he often makes me feel like I'm his only client. It is a privilege to work with not only a talented man, but a godly one.

Coming Soon
From Thor Ramsey

TO

NOTHING

BE

THE

GLORY

THOR

RAMSEY

A comedian engages the culture of unbelief

The René Descartes Joke Edition

The Comical Nature of Atheism

Read an excerpt from *To Nothing Be the Glory*

C H A P T E R   6

——————— ❧ ———————

Penn & Teller's Magic of Skepticism
(The Punchline That Doesn't Exist)

D riving to Las Vegas from southern California only takes about three and a half hours and one speeding ticket. During the drive, I notice the scenery is missing. That's really the only way to describe Nevada, a state that makes Arizona appear fertile. It's like the state gambled away all its cacti. I'm driving to Vegas, Baby, Vegas to interview the atheist comedy-magicians Penn & Teller, not that they've agreed to the interview. Like a good Christian, I'm going to ambush them. So, before I leave, I place a Jesus-fish eating a Darwin-fish on my bumper.

Penn & Teller's management told my literary agent that they only do taped interviews, meaning something that's going to be on film or television. If only we were making a documentary. My iPhone has a camera and I have a YouTube account, but this didn't seem to matter to them. My lit agent emailed them back and forth several times. I followed-up with an email myself that shot for being cordial. The answer was still "no thanks." We thought of saying that I was a rock journalist with *Rolling Stone* magazine who was doing a piece on celebrity atheists, but we thought this might be construed as lying since none of it was true.

However, all was not lost. After every show for the last 9 years, Penn & Teller stand in the lobby signing autographs, meeting their fans and getting their pictures taken with mild-mannered Christians who offer them pocket Bibles. This was our chance. Our strategy was to wait until the line had nearly died down and then while I shook

Penn's hand, my lit agent would take our photo while I subtly asked him a question.

Penn & Teller are the magic and comedy duo who became nationally known in the late 1980's by appearing regularly on *The Late Show with David Letterman*, back when it was a late show. One of them (Penn) is tall, husky and talks during their sets while the other (Teller) is short, impish and silent. Penn talks a lot. Teller never talks. Their tricks are sometimes fake-blood gory, using chainsaws, swords, catching bullets in their teeth – that kind of thing. But they have always dressed dapperly, like two men late for a wedding. They are both atheists. The one who talks, Penn Jillette, is an outspoken atheist. Probably because of the talking thing. He even wrote a book about atheism called *God, No!* (I was tempted to write "he penned a book," because, you know, his name... forget it.) Penn Jillette has rippled long black hair that looks like it could clutch you by the throat and make you sit down and shut up all by itself. Note to self: Proceed with caution during the interview.

Once I arrive in Vegas, Marshall, my literary agent/editor/Las Vegas handler, says he wants me to have the full Vegas experience: "I thought we'd go for one of the last Vegas meal deals. A thick steak for $5.99."

At a casino, of course.

The Ellis Island Casino, which was an odd name for a casino I thought, but accurate nonetheless because it appeared that many of the patrons should have been quarantined. Or at least given a separate room where they could blow smoke out of their nostrils (something I didn't even know people did anymore) without having to endure my California smoke-free look of disdain. The steak was only $5.99. We decided to endure the smoke. The cleaning bill to get the smell out of our clothing was $9.98, but a deal's a deal.

Whatever the name of the restaurant at the Ellis Island Casino (I think it was called "Restaurant"), the decor was "deadheading back home because I couldn't get a load." Truck-stop circa 1978. The steaks were piping hot and without any seasoning, just the right amount of blandness. And after a 30-minute wait, it turns out they were $6.99.

Welcome to Vegas.

What's the best way to describe downtown Las Vegas?

Let's say you're driving down a dirt road at around twenty-miles per hour. Sitting in the passenger seat next to you is a shapely young lady in an expensive black negligee who opens her car door, jumps out and rolls into the ditch. After she crawls out of the ditch – that's Las Vegas.

Penn & Teller's theater is at the Rio, a stark contrast to the Ellis Island Casino and their $6.99 steaks. The difference between the Rio and the establishment where we acquired gastro intestinal difficulties can best be described this way: the girl sitting in the passenger seat never jumps out of the car. The theater seats are comfortable and velvety red with seventy-percent capacity on a weeknight. While perusing the program, I noticed under the "Thank You" section they listed Mac King, a comedy-magician who I worked with years ago. I should have called Mac King. Maybe he could have arranged the interview.

The lights blink, theater sign language for the show's about to begin.

In his "This I Believe" segment for National Public Radio, Penn described his atheism as informing every moment of his life. It certainly informed the show in Vegas that night. There were several points in the show where Penn said things like, "All miracles are a hoax, a fabrication, a trick by liars and cheats and swindlers. And I know them all." Anti-supernaturalism informed their show, which is a very Age of Enlightenment thing to have influencing your show. Anything that is seen to violate the laws of nature would be considered a miracle. Penn's hair, for example.

But when it comes to miracles, I don't really think they are the issue here. The issue is that Penn, Teller and I have a different worldview. In Teller's worldview, objectivism is the reason for everything good. In Penn's worldview, all miracles are tricks. In my worldview, if God exists, he can do whatever he wants. *Can God create a rock that he can't lift?* God can do anything that he wants. But he doesn't want to create a rock that he can't lift because that would be irrational. God doesn't want to do anything that violates his nature and character. He wouldn't do anything of the sort. *So, God can't do anything?* Nope. Not if it violates who he is. God is not man that he would hope to be something other than who he actually is. You get the idea. That's what it means to be God.

We all start with preconceived notions, but reasoning must start somewhere. It's not arbitrary. No one does a card trick with a blank deck. Even Penn & Teller will tell you that. We have to start with what we know to be true (with what the brilliant philosopher Alvin Plantinga calls basic beliefs) and work from there. The goal is to align all of our notions with the truth, not rationalize our worldview with slight of mind.

Let's use one of their tricks to illustrate this (as I adopt a pastoral tone).

During one trick, Teller held up a rose petal, its long shadow clearly seen in the background. When he cut the shadow of the rose petal, the actual rose petal fell off. It's a great trick, because you say to yourself, "Either something miraculous happened or I've witnessed a great trick." Being a reasonable person, I surmise that I witnessed a trick, because miracles don't cost $45 per person.

This is what I know to be true. I am at a magic show. Magic in our culture no longer carries with it the idea of mysterious supernatural forces. Nowadays, we know that magic is trickery. Therefore, based upon the context of our culture and the $45 ticket in my pocket, I objectively deduce that I witnessed a trick, not a miracle. But does the fact that our culture no longer believes in real magic mean there is no such thing as real magic?

To serve as a further illustration, let's say that after the show Penn's hair strangles me for conducting an unauthorized interview. I am dead. The paramedics come and pronounce me dead. Marshall realizes he will never get his $45 back for buying my ticket. Right then, he prays that God would perform a miracle and raise me from the dead. The next day, I'm back at the show. Penn & Teller claim that the paramedics must have made a mistake, as did the hospital, as did the morgue.

But there I am, flesh and blood, enjoying a good fire eating routine, yet they will not have it. There is no good reason to believe that God did not perform a miracle, other than the fact that their worldview just won't allow it. That's the only thing they have to bank on. It's the most common argument against miracles: We know they can't happen.

This argument is really a philosophical sleight of hand: miracles don't happen because we know they can't. They don't believe in miracles because their worldview says not to. You may level the charge of circular reasoning against such a claim, but alas, all systems of belief are circular in nature, even ones that base themselves upon evidentiary claims. Maybe you claim to have a scientific worldview, thus you contend, "I can only believe what can be proven." And why is that? "Because I have a scientific worldview." Watch out for your butt, because you just circled around.

Maybe your worldview is postmodern, thus you would never claim anything, but you might say very softly, "One cannot ever really know anything for sure." And why is that? "I don't know for sure." Okay, go get in line with the agnostics.

Another claims, "I only believe what is completely reasonable to believe." Why? "Because I believe in reason." All belief systems are circular in nature.

"I do not believe God is there." Why? "Because I have not seen Him." Somewhere there is an atheist with a dog chasing its tail.

The reality is that we all begin with premises. Then you begin to build your beliefs upon your premise, which is why your beliefs naturally lead back to your premise. As theologian and philosopher John Frame explains, "One who believes that human reason is the ultimate standard can argue that view only by appealing to reason. One who believes that the Bible is the ultimate standard can argue only by appealing to the Bible. Since all positions partake equally of circularity at this level, it cannot be a point of criticism against any of them."[12]

---

12 John M. Frame, "Presuppositional Apologetics," *Frame & Poythress*, http://www.frame-poythress.org/presuppositional-apologetics/

The tragedy is not the circular nature of Penn & Teller's viewpoint, but its limitation is what is tragic, this worldview that doesn't allow for the miraculous.

This is the kicker to me, though. Even the live tricks that Penn & Teller performed that night in Las Vegas pale in comparison to merely the descriptions of the miracles that Jesus performed in the gospels. When a miracle that's written is more engaging than a live performance, well, that says something about the miracle. But miracles always trump tricks.

Maybe church should have a cover charge.

Say $45.

After the show, we head to our interview. That is, we get in line with all their fans. We get in the very back of the line in the off chance that the interview goes really well. We don't want to hold up the line. That and I want to delay the possible disappointment if Jillette just rolls his eyes at me. This has been a long day already. Most people are not this committed to being blown off, but here I stand.

Finally, when I stand before Penn, I ask him, "In your opinion, what's the most positive thing that atheism has brought to the world?" He seemed a little prickly, not generally, but with me specifically. Maybe because he'd already declined to be interviewed by me. Twice. Maybe because I interviewed him anyway. Maybe because my literary agent/editor/Las Vegas handler decided to stand behind me feverishly taking notes on his notepad instead of flipping on his tape recorder.

Jillette stands 6 feet 6 inches with all the twitches of a charging bull who's been hooked by a matador. In short, he's intimidating. I stand 6 feet 0 inches according to my driver's license, 5 feet 11 inches according to the mug shot, possibly 6 inches from nose to ground after this interview.

He stepped back, looked down at me (his only option) and said loud enough for the few people remaining to hear, "DNA..." I thought that was it, end of ambush interview. Then he continued, ever so slightly perturbed, "Yeah, DNA will save the world. There's also Norman Borlaug who was responsible for saving over 50 million lives, the most people saved by anyone." I couldn't assume this was a subtle jab at Jesus who is also reputed to have saved more people than anyone in the world, because Jillette didn't know me from Adam.

He continued, "Richard Feynman. Darwin. 70 percent of Noble Prize winners since its inception. How many more do you want? The list goes on."

At this point, he was backing away, ready to use his Sharpie to sign someone's program or tag my forehead with a large check-mark to warn Teller.

Teller, the silent half of Penn & Teller, was not only signing autographs after the show, he was talking to people. With his voice. The man talks. I had mixed emotions about him breaking character. I never even imagined that I would have a chance to interview Teller. Did Harpo Marx talk in public? Did Harpo ever break character? I don't know. So, I called my friend, comedian Joby Saad, who is an unofficial Marx Brother's scholar. He is only unofficial because he has no degree and is unknown in the circles of academia.

According to Joby: "Harpo never broke character. But in real life no one could tell the Marx brothers apart. That's why they created such distinct characters. Since they all looked so much alike they could change costumes and no one knew the difference during a live performance. Occasionally, Harpo would be Chico and Chico would be Harpo."

Does Teller know?

The crowd around Teller had dissipated, so I walked over and shook his hand while asking, "Out of curiosity, are you an atheist too?"

"Of course," he said, like who isn't an atheist. Or "of course" like, "What else could I be and hang out with Penn? Have you seen that guy? He's intimidating. His bangs alone could beat me unconscious."

Then I asked him the same question, "What's the most positive contribution atheism has made to the world?"

"Well, atheism is just a subset of objectivism. And objectivism is responsible for everything that is good."

Yes, this from a Las Vegas showman.

Teller seemed open to more questions, so I asked him, "What's the most negative thing that atheism has brought to the world?"

He said, "Nothing. Theism is responsible for a lot of bad stuff. Whenever you involve gods bad things happen."

This is something I've noticed from being around many atheists of late, they use the word "gods" instead of saying, "God." I can only assume this is because the term "gods" is more generic and because polytheism (the belief in multiple gods) was discredited eons ago. When an atheist uses the word "God" we all know who he's talking about. It's not an atheist's goal to give credit where credit is due.

"Okay, tell me this," I said. "If you could recommend only one book by an atheist what would it be?"

"Anything by Ayn Rand," he said, which really surprised me. That same week, I was in the middle of the book *The Age of American Unreason* by freethinking skeptic and Pulitzer Prize finalist Susan Jacoby. In the book, Jacoby was rather dismissive of Rand, at least, it seems that way when she writes, "Forgotten in their original form but not gone, the worst pseudoscientific ideas emanating from the late nineteenth century are constantly being marketed under new brand names in the United States. Social Darwinism has never died: it manifested itself as a bulwark of eugenics until the Second World War; in the tedious midcentury 'objectivist' philosophy of Ayn Rand."

Now, I'm no New York intellectual (probably because of the time difference), but that seems rather negative to me.

It was at this point that Teller, who was very mild-mannered and seemed legitimately interested in what people had to say, complemented me on my choice of eye-wear.

"Those are cool glasses," he said.

"Thank you. My children made them. We're homeschoolers."

I was just about to ask him the same two questions regarding Christianity when he noticed Marshall, my literary agent/editor/Las Vegas handler writing speedily on his notepad. We had a little tape recorder, but it's not nice to record people without their consent. So,

Marshall thought he would just write everything down in front of him.

"Who are you guys?" Teller asked.

Penn just happened to be walking by at that moment and he said to me, "Hey, your modifier is in the wrong place."

He could see the confusion on my face, so he clarified, "That photo of the nuns on your website."

On my website there was a photo (I don't recall where I came across it) of ten nuns who were each holding shotguns. The caption below read, "Much to their surprise, the Virgins awaiting Muslims in heaven were not quite what they expected." The sentence is grammatically incorrect because the word "their" is modifying the word "virgins" instead of "Muslims." This is also something that annoys me, but I give punch lines and dialogue creative license. Whoever wrote this should have just dropped the words "much to their surprise" and the sentence would be fine. If that's the worst thing he can say about my website, I'm okay with that. Still, I'll be deleting it or at least footnoting Penn Jillette's keen eye for grammar.[13] God is in the details, after all.

"Oh," I said, not expecting that Penn Jillette would check my website for grammatical errors. Maybe his crack about who saved the most people in the world *was* intentional. That's amazing. I think I was just mocked by Penn Jillette. What a blessing, because how many Christians can say that? Oh, right. All of us. But mine was *personal,* so there.

"You gotta watch that [expletive]," he said while walking backward.

Life is meaningless because there is no God, but that's no reason for bad grammar.

After his remark, both Penn & Teller, the Las Vegas magicians and illusionists, disappeared. Marshall and I stood staring at each other, taking in the moment as the last two fans standing in the lobby.

---

13 Penn Jillette has a keen eye for grammar.

"He checked out my website," I said, my egotism unbecoming as always.

"Well, that explains why they declined the interview."

If everyone's a comedian, does that make the existence of God more likely or less likely?

Like most people walking to their car after a Las Vegas magic show, our thoughts lent themselves to the philosophy of objectivism. Let's take a moment and break down objectivism, the philosophy created by novelist Ayn Rand. Objectivism says that there is objective reality that doesn't depend upon any of us. Whether you believe it or not, it is real. It's outside of you. There is real reality.

Agreed.

Rand's objectivism sounds a lot like logical positivism, which says only positive statements that can be proved true or false are meaningful. Everything else is mere opinion.[14] Rand's objectivism asserts that you can *only* discover reality through investigation by using reason and logical thinking skills alone. There is no other way to discover reality. That is, unless, people are blind to certain aspects of reality. "If you can't show it to me, it doesn't exist" is a limiting way to view life. It's very much in line with scientism, which says that we can only know what science discovers. Everything else is speculation, like dead matter becoming conscious of itself. Pure speculation. Nothing scientific about that.

Most importantly, objectivism says that the main purpose of life is the happiness of all sentient beings. Naturally, such a philosophy would lead to the belief that selfishness is virtuous, which is what Rand believed.

This is my stop.

"Whatever makes you happy" doesn't work as a philosophy in real life. The pedophile is doing "whatever makes him happy." Now, either pedophilia is objectively wrong, meaning it's wrong whether you believe it's wrong, or not. In other words, in real reality, it's wrong.

---

14 Horton, "The Christian Mind," (October 15, 2014).

Even if society begins to embrace pedophilia as a relationship option, it is still objectively wrong and will always be objectively wrong, progressive politicians notwithstanding.

But to say anything is wrong (or right) there has to be an objective source from which this rightness or wrongness originates. This objective source would be an unseen reality with an intrinsic authority to define values that transcends all human authority to define values. (I'm hinting around about God here.) All that to say, just because something makes you happy doesn't mean it's right. Therefore, your happiness or the happiness of any sentient being cannot be the ultimate purpose in life. Unless there is no objective source for right or wrong. Then, by all means, whatever makes you happy. But just remember, it's whatever makes *anyone* happy, including NAMBLA, the group that endorses adult men having sex with young boys. But if that is the case, then whatever makes you unhappy doesn't matter either, because whatever makes you happy is bound to make someone else unhappy. *Don't you have a mother?*

Now, I know that you might be screaming that this example is too extreme, that atheists don't endorse pedophilia. (Yeah, I said it.) You tell me that this idea of the happiness of all sentient beings has a footnote. The footnote being that you can do whatever makes you happy, let's all say it together now, "As long as you're not hurting anyone." Clearly, pedophiles are hurtful. It can be safely said that the average atheist is for gay-rights, but opposed to pedophilia and for the principle reason that one is seen as harmful and the other is not. But isn't this standard of happiness arbitrary?

"No, it's based upon reason," you say. (And if not, just go with me. I'm doing my best to involve you in this discussion.)

Then let's go to reason (assuming that reason itself is not an arbitrary construct) and answer this question, "Who decides what is hurtful?"

In a very interesting (though it's not good beach reading) book by Steven Smith called *The Disenchantment of Secular Discourse,* he explains this little thing called the Harm Principle. The Harm Principle in popular culture is stated as such, "You can do whatever you want, as long as you're not hurting anyone." The problem with this truism is that it's false, or at least so utterly subjective that it becomes a useless and immeasurable standard. Okay, I'll stick with false.

Again, who decides what is harmful? You can claim that watching porn in the privacy of your own home is not harming anyone. Personally, I'm already a little emotionally distraught having to block out an image of you sitting in a recliner without any pants on. And I don't even know you. This harm thing is trickier than we realize.

What you do in private reveals something about you. In fact, who you are in private is closest to who you really are, so what you do in private always makes its way back into public. Mr. Smith explains, "Our movie-watching habits will affect how we talk, how we spend our time, what activities we choose to engage in and support: while we are watching adult films behind closed curtains we are not attending the high school musical or the baseball game... what we do in private will almost certainly have a gradual and subtle, but very real, influence on the sort of community all of us experience."[15]

Never buy a used recliner.

The Harm Principle becomes a very subjective enterprise where anyone and everyone can claim they are being harmed in some way. And vice versa, that what they are doing is not harming anyone, but this is a purely subjective claim. You cannot foresee the far reaching influence of your various behaviors. Who knows how you personally have affected the young women in porn films by supporting this industry. Maybe a young girl is molested as a child by a neighborhood boy a few years older. As she grows into puberty her image of sexuality is marred by this incident. Soon, she is exploited by another man who introduces her to the porn industry where she makes films. She wishes she were not the way she is, but she can't seem to find a way out. And there you are paying for porn, indirectly keeping her

---

15 Steven D. Smith, *The Disenchantment of Secular Discourse* (Harvard University Press, 2010), 85-86

in bondage by supporting the porn industry. No, you're no hurting anyone. Not you.

These are very difficult waters to tread without some objective standard of harm. Whenever we begin to talk about harm and "our rights" we move in a metaphysical and theological direction. Claiming any rights in an absolute way is affirming the existence of God,[16] otherwise the rights are arbitrary and can be tossed aside. *Just put it in that pile of constructs over there.* So, is pedophilia always and absolutely wrong or is it dependent upon some subjective standard of happiness? What if there are young boys (as the pedophiles claim) who want these relationships? What if some young boys find happiness in this? Is there an objective standard or not?

Real reality says there is a Creator who defines all things. He is the Definer of the stars above, the inventor of the laws of physics beneath, the source of the moral law within, the sustainer of you and me here and now, everything that has breath and everything inanimate was created by this one who is other than we are in every way. He has given definition and value to everything, which means we are not the definers of anything. We don't create value or give things meaning. This leaves us only one alternative – discovery. We can discover how he has revealed himself and defined everything according to his Word, the Bible; or we can resist reality.

I hope you don't wait for the great tiebreaker, because like Penn & Teller after the show's over, God is going to meet every one of his fans and every one of his detractors.

Whether you believe it or not.

Objectivism at its best.

ॐ

To Nothing Be the Glory is coming soon. Sign up for Thor's email list at www.thorramsey.com to be notified when it's released.

---

16 This is writer Greg Forster's thought, but I don't remember where I read it.

ABOUT THE AUTHOR

Thor Ramsey is married to a woman and has written several books and one screenplay that was made into a movie (*Youth Group*). He's written other screenplays that sit unnoticed in the digital world of his laptop.

He planted a church in 2016 called Center Church (www.center-church.life) and as of this writing it is still in existence.

In addition to hunting and sailing, there are many other things he never does. Though, on occasion, like at the end of books, he enjoys writing about himself in the third person.